Hard Luck Coast

The Perilous Reefs
of Point Montara

To June —

Thanks for sharing the voyage.

John S.

HARD LUCK COAST

THE PERILOUS REEFS OF POINT MONTARA

BY

JOANN SEMONES

THE GLENCANNON PRESS

El Cerrito
2010

Published by The Glencannon Press
Tel. 800-711-8985, Fax. 510-528-3194
www.glencannon.com

The photograph on the cover is courtesy of Julie Barrow. The illustration used on the endpapers is courtesy of the author.

First Edition, second printing.

ISBN 978-1-889901-51-0

Library of Congress Cataloging-in-Publication Data

Semones, JoAnn, 1945-
    Hard luck coast : the perilous reefs of Point Montara / by JoAnn Semones. -- 1st ed.
        p. cm.
    Includes bibliographical references and index.
    ISBN 978-1-889901-51-0 (alk. paper)
1. Shipwrecks--California--Montara, Point--History. 2. Montara, Point (Calif.)--
History, Naval. I. Title
    F868.S19S45 2010
    979.4'69--dc22
                                                            2010003791

Publisher's note: Every effort is made to obtain and reproduce the best quality photographs. Due to the age of the photos available, some are of a lesser quality. They have nevertheless been used.

DEDICATION

For Julie Barrow,
who is my guiding light.

ACKNOWLEDGEMENTS

In writing a book about shipwrecks, the sea provides the inspiration and the ships tell the story. Yet, it is the people, both past and present that bring the two together.

Praise goes to archivists Mary Gibson of the Maine Maritime Museum, Claudia Jew of the Mariners Museum in Newport News, Virginia, Carol Peterson of the San Mateo County History Museum and to Christopher Bauman of Point Montara Lighthouse for digging deep into their resources and offering their valuable knowledge.

Special thanks go to Marvin and Ressa Fairbanks, John E. Gonzales, Jr., George H. Graham, Robert Hanssen, Christopher Lindstrom, Pat Long, Carl W. May, Mike Royden, Michael Simpson, and Arthur H. Smith, Jr. for generously contributing their memories and family photographs. These threads of daily life are precious threads in the fabric of maritime lore.

I am indebted to Allen Bunes and Shannon Nottestad for unselfishly sharing coastal artist Galen Wolf's unpublished stories and artwork. His *Legends of the Coastland* add a unique dimension to local history.

My heartfelt appreciation goes to Shelley Rose and Capt. Walter Jaffee, who fuel my enthusiasm and share my love of the sea, its ships, and its ever fascinating stories.

Most especially, my eternal gratitude goes to Julie Barrow, who willingly continues to be my fellow history detective and eager research companion, avid book-signing and road-trip cohort, chief editor and patient reader, foremost cheerleader, and life partner.

Thank you for weathering all the stormy seas and staying true to the course.

– J.A.S.

CONTENTS

ILLUSTRATIONS

PROLOGUE

The rugged California coast has a vivid and colorful tale to tell. Centuries of her story are chronicled through the shipwrecks scattered below the ocean's surface. Vessels of exploration, commerce, travel, and trade have all yielded their contents to the sea, sometimes tragically, sometimes strangely opportune.

This companion volume to *Shipwrecks, Scalawags, and Scavengers: The Storied Waters of Pigeon Point*, shares more of these elusive adventures. *Hard Luck Coast: The Perilous Reefs of Point Montara*, dips under the sea once again, bringing more than a dozen additional stories to light.

JoAnn Semones' attention to detail has carried her from coast to coast conducting research. She has sifted through the treasures hidden in numerous and sometimes obscure maritime archives, gathering rare images and long-forgotten lore. She's also discovered and interviewed ancestors of the characters whose lives and misfortunes are captured within these pages.

Enjoy a peek through the window of time, viewing the unique maritime history that lays beneath waters protected by NOAA's National Marine Sanctuary Program.

Dawn Hayes
Education & Outreach Coordinator
Monterey Bay National Marine Sanctuary Program
National Oceanic & Atmospheric Administration

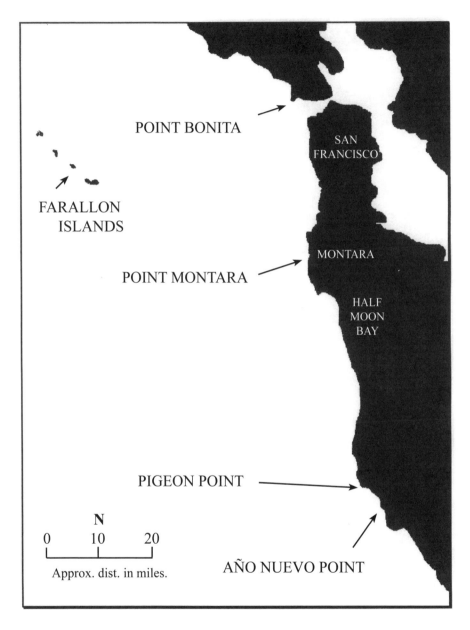

POINT BONITA

SAN
FRANCISCO

FARALLON
ISLANDS

MONTARA

POINT MONTARA

HALF
MOON
BAY

PIGEON POINT

N

0   10   20

Approx. dist. in miles.

AÑO NUEVO POINT

The central coast of California.
Courtesy of Janet Taggart.

INTRODUCTION

Nestled along the central coast of California, the picturesque hamlets of Montara, twenty miles south of San Francisco, and neighboring Half Moon Bay, five miles farther to the south, are kindred communities. They share geographic boundaries, a common lore, and strong ties to the past.

The region's earliest inhabitants were a band of Indians called the Chiguan. These Native Americans, today known as the Ohlone, settled here over 5,800 years ago.

Wildlife and marine life were as plentiful as they were diverse. Deer, elk, bear, and wildfowl roamed the land. Trout, salmon, shellfish, and sea mammals filled the surrounding waters.

When Spanish missionaries arrived in the mid-1700s, the region was used by their Mission Dolores in San Francisco to graze large herds of cattle, horses, and oxen. After land grants were given to Spanish soldiers and civil leaders in the 1840s, the area was carved into several huge parcels, each consisting of thousands of acres of prime coastland.

The southern portion, originally called San Benito and later Spanishtown, developed as the first real town in San Mateo County. In 1874, the city was renamed Half Moon Bay after the concave shape of the coast that forms its western border. The northern portion grew more slowly, sprinkled mostly with produce farms and dairies. Known as Montara by 1875, it was established as a fog signal station after several ships wrecked nearby.

California Writer John Steinbeck referred to the treacherous strip of shore between Montara and Half Moon Bay as "the hard luck coast." Along this foggy, final approach to San Francisco, vessels were forced to hug the perilous shoreline, putting them in danger of its rocky outcroppings and unruly seas.

A kerosene lantern was installed to light the way for seafarers in 1900, followed by a skeleton tower in 1912. This was replaced by the current tower in 1928. At first glance, Point Montara Lighthouse seems unassuming. Standing only thirty feet tall, its tiny stature belies a rich and adventurous maritime heritage. Having stood on the Atlantic and Pacific Coast, the tower is America's only beacon to have witnessed shipwrecks on two shores.

From 1851 to 1946, dozens of ships sank in the notorious corridor between Montara and Half Moon Bay. Each shipwreck represents a separate, yet integrated piece of history, linking us to the past. Each lighthouse, whether it contains a small lantern or a giant first order Fresnel lens, is a mighty monument to that past. Their beacons are our eyes to the world as it was, attesting to the stories of irreplaceable people, places, and times. What follows are those stories.

1

MUTINY AND MURDER

JANUARY 8, 1856

Classed as "a very fast bark with clipper lines," the *Isabelita Hyne* is the first recorded shipwreck in Half Moon Bay. The vessel's strange demise raised questions of mutiny and murder.

China Trade

As early as the 1600s, European ships carried a myriad of exotic goods from the Orient. Popular treasures included dried coconut (known as copra) used to make oil; chinoiserie such as silk, porcelain, gold, ivory, jade, pearls, and gemstones; mercury, ginger, and cowrie shells. This soon gave rise to the term "China trade."

American ships began to compete in the lucrative China trade in the 1830s. Porcelain, which had been so common in China that it was used as ballast in some ships, was snapped up by wealthy Americans for their parlors and dining rooms. They craved other artifacts, too, including bamboo, silk, incense, fans, lacquer ware, objects d'art, and firecrackers.

However, it was tea, popular in both America and Great Britain, and the enormous profits to be made from it, that set off a headlong burst of shipping competition. The trade was so profitable that twenty

In the 1850s, ships like the Isabelita Hyne *carried tea and exotic wares from China to San Francisco and other American ports.* Peabody Essex Museum.

Early American mariners, such as this one, traveled the "Silk Road of the Sea" connecting the Far East with the Western World. Museum of American China Trade.

million pounds of tea passed through Canton annually. By the 1840s, tea remained the heart of the trade, accounting for eighty percent of China's exports. "America's thirst for Chinese tea," one trader declared, "remained strong for a very long time."

By mid-century, American tastes were becoming more sophisticated, preferring the freshest tea, and they willingly paid a huge premium for the first shipment of the season. This was the incentive that led shipping merchants to charter the fastest vessels. Swift, fine-lined ships such as the *Isabelita Hyne* were employed and some made the voyage from Canton to New York in as little as seventy-four days.

Canton, located eighty miles from the sea on the banks of the Pearl River, was China's most important seaport for close to two thousand years. Descriptions of the beauty of the lush, tropical nature of the area often refer to "pearly waters and white clouds." It was also the starting port of the "Silk Road on the Sea," an extensive network of trade routes connecting the Far East with the Western world.

Very Fast Sailer

Originally designed for the Rio de Janeiro trade, the *Isabelita Hyne* rapidly gained the reputation as "a very fast sailer, besides being very staunch." Built by J.K. Hammils of Philadelphia, Pennsylvania in 1848, the 350-ton bark was 114 feet long, nearly 16 feet wide, and was fastened with copper throughout. The vessel made numerous voyages to Brazil delivering assorted cargo, returning safely laden with sugar and coffee.

Words from a poem entitled "Trust the Winds O' Sailor" by Kathy Huebner could have been written for the adventurous little ship: "Many a day she's gone out to sea; exploring the world, trading goods, (far from) the land; may (she) provide you courage and support by command."

She also made two voyages from New York to San Francisco. The first was a 125-day journey with Capt. Samuel F. Dewing from January 12, 1851 to May 18, 1851. The second voyage was made in 124 days with a Capt. Lamson from September 8, 1852 to January 10, 1853.

The *Isabelita Hyne* turned her sails toward the Far East when her owners, Nye, Parkin & Company of Baltimore, Maryland found pressing commercial needs for the ship in the Orient. Observers claimed that the slim-hulled, fast little bark "ran more China trade from 1853 to 1856 than any other vessel of her tonnage."

Philadelphia Harbor as it appeared in the 1840s when the Isabelita Hyne *was built.*
Library of Congress.

The driving force behind the enterprise was Gideon Nye, Jr. Born in 1808 in Acushnet, Massachusetts, about three miles east of New Bedford, Nye left for China in 1833. "The very name of China," he wrote later, "was, at that day, pregnant of the romance of history, and suggested imaginative dreams."

After serving as a tea trader in Canton, Nye followed his dreams and established the trading firm of Nye, Parkin & Company in 1843. With growing interests in China as well as in America, the firm became Nye Brothers in 1853. "He was a bold and extensive operator in the Chinese-American trade," newspapers reported. "He amassed a fortune of about $6,000,000."

Unfortunately, having overextended its resources, Nye's firm collapsed in 1856. He moved to Macao, about sixty-five miles south of Canton and forty miles from Hong Kong, where he became active in politics. Nye was one of a group of influential Americans proposing that the United States seize and annex the island of Formosa in 1857. Working through personal contacts, he spared no effort to gain the attention of high U.S. government officials to try to win support for the scheme.

Although the plan failed, Nye's efforts made him a well-known figure in the Far East. From 1858 to 1863, he served as American Deputy Consul and then American Vice Consul of Macao. After writing several books about China, Nye died in Canton in 1888.

"The death of this venerable resident, who had for fifty-five years been identified with the best interests of the community in Southern China, caused a deep sorrow among those who had long known him as an amiable gentleman of varied experience, refinement, noble purpose, and fine talents," an obituary read. "The flags of the consulates, custom house, and foreign ships in port were at half mast two days in token of public esteem."

The Wreck

Along with losing his business, Nye lost his most profitable ship in 1856. Bound for San Francisco from Hong Kong on her fateful voyage, the *Isabelita Hyne* was carrying a cargo of tea, sugar, rice, and silks valued at $120,000. At 10:00 P.M. on January 8th, the bark foundered near Half Moon Bay, California. Although the cause of the mishap was never determined, some speculated that the wreck was not accidental.

Gideon Nye, Jr., who owned the Isabelita Hyne, *was a well-known figure in the Far East.* Whaling Museum of New Bedford.

Shortly after the *Isabelita Hyne* grounded, a reporter for the *Daily California Chronicle* claimed that he received a bizarre tip. According to him, an "intelligent seafaring man who had communication with persons from the wreck," accused the crew of a brutal conspiracy. "There was a mutiny," he blustered. "The captain and mate were murdered and the crew intentionally wrecked their vessel to conceal evidence of their crime."

There was also an alarming rumor that the dead body of Capt. Calhoun, the *Isabelita Hyne*'s master, had been lashed to some of the rigging with his head cut off. "The captain and mate are missing and all accounts which we have of the cause and manner of the wreck are unsatisfactory," the reporter asserted. "The cabin is high and dry and was visited by some boatmen. They found no charts, no papers, no compass, no clothes, and the bulkhead was broken in, evidently by human hands."

Other rumors swirled around the wreck. Initially, the bark's cargo was thought to have been scavenged, at least in part, by local residents. Some accounts insisted, "Residents of the neighborhood of Half Moon Bay had been guilty of pillaging the wreck and appropriating whatever had washed ashore."

However, James Denniston, who owned four miles of coastal land where the *Isabelita Hyne* ran ashore, claimed that the vessel had not been looted. "On the contrary," reports said, "he placed his entire force of men and Indians together with his animals at the disposal of those who were endeavoring to offer relief to the persons and property of the disabled vessel."

Whatever the truth was, little remained to salvage. According to the *Daily Alta*, the ship's hull, sails, rigging, anchor, chains, and other materials were sold for a mere forty dollars on January 16th by T.L. Poulfere & Company, auctioneers; John C. Boyt, agent and underwriters; and McCondray & Co., consignors.

The Findings

Within days of the wreck, "a portion" of Capt. Calhoun's body washed ashore, along with the remains of the first mate, Beatty. Also recovered was the ship's log which indicated the captain had been ill for more than half of the seventy-day passage. After completing an examination of the bodies in San Francisco, Coroner Kent found no evidence of foul play.

Somehow, the remaining crew of the *Isabelita Hyne* scrambled ashore and surfaced in San Francisco. On January 18th, they appeared before U.S. Commissioner John A. Monroe to give testimony regarding the incident. Although reports of the commissioner's findings are vague, "all crew agreed to the manner of the wreck. The captain and mate were both distinctly seen on board the vessel after she struck."

Weakened by his illness, no doubt Capt. Calhoun was unable to cope with the sudden shock of an unexpected shipwreck. First Mate Beatty, who "is supposed to have had all his money on his person," apparently drowned by its weight when he was thrown overboard by a lurch of the ship.

The commissioner also dismissed accounts concerning the absence of the vessel's charts, papers, and instruments as "without foundation." Neither had the bulwark of the cabin been broken in "by human hands" as reported.

Amid the drama and controversy surrounding the mishap, the *Isabelita Hyne* was nearly forgotten. For two weeks, the abandoned ship lay beaten continuously by savage breakers. Ultimately, one newspaper noted, "The vessel has entirely disappeared, having been broken up by the force of the sea."

All that remains is the mystery of how she came to be wrecked.

2

BITTERSWEET ENDING

JANUARY 10, 1862

During America's Civil War, the Peruvian schooner *Elfin A. Kniper* provided a vital commercial link to the West Coast. On a stormy, wintry evening, that link was severed.

Sugar Trade

In 1862, America was in the throes of a bloody Civil War. President Abraham Lincoln had ordered a blockade of Southern ports, drastically affecting that area's shipment of many crucial goods, including sugar.

One of the states hit hardest by the blockade was Louisiana. During the forty years preceding the Civil War, Louisiana produced no less than ninety-five percent of the nation's sugar crop. As the war dragged on, the sugar industry would be decimated.

Ships were scarce, making it difficult to distribute the crop, banks curtailed credit, and provisions were in short supply. Union soldiers destroyed sugar fields, looted plantations, and seized food and livestock. Slaves, the sugar industry's primary labor force, left plantations in droves. "Many fine plantations," the *New Orleanian* newspaper remarked, "are now lying waste and idle."

During the Civil War, President Abraham Lincoln ordered a blockade of southern ports, drastically affecting the area's economy. Author's collection.

After Louisiana sugar plantations fell into ruin, Americans relied on the Elfin A. Kniper *and other ships to deliver sugar from Peru.* Author's collection.

Of the 2,400 sugar producers in the state on the eve of war in 1861, less than two hundred farms would still cultivate cane by 1864. The value of the sugar industry would fall from $200,000,000 to no more than $30,000,000 in 1865. Although sugarcane survived, production would not match previous levels for twenty-five years.

Throughout the war, the U.S. turned to other countries to supply its needs. Laying 4,000 miles south of California, Peru became a significant source of sugar. The chief characteristic which distinguished the Peruvian sugar industry from its counterparts elsewhere in the world was the absence of seasonality in production. Sugar in Peru could be harvested year round, and favorable ecological conditions resulted in exceptionally high yields.

The origins of the sugar industry in Peru go back to the latter part of the sixteenth century when production was first introduced in the fertile river valleys of the otherwise barren, desert-like north coast by Spanish colonists. Cultivation of sugarcane was labor intensive and time consuming. Planters frequently complained about the inefficiency and expense of using oxen-driven plows to harvest the fields.

In the 1850s, technological advances such as steam powered mills and burgeoning markets turned Peru decisively toward overseas sugar exports. The opening of the British market to foreign sugar stimulated demand and prices rose accordingly an average of four percent annually. By the 1860s, schooners like the *Elfin A. Kniper* were carrying sugar to ports worldwide.

Revenue Cutter Service

To enforce President Lincoln's blockade of Confederate ports, the U.S. naval fleet was divided into four major commands. The Atlantic coast from Virginia to Key West was covered by the North and South Atlantic Blockading Squadrons. The East and West Blockading Squadrons covered the Gulf of Mexico coast from Key West to Brownville, Texas. "With only forty-two ships," one source acknowledged, "it quickly became apparent that the strength of the Navy was inadequate for the new and varied duties imposed by the war."

The U.S. Revenue Cutter Service, usually assigned to deter smuggling and enforce customs laws as well as to assist mariners in need, augmented the Navy's efforts. At the time, the Cutter Service consisted of a mere twenty-eight vessels. "You will cooperate," President Lincoln ordered the Secretary of the Treasury, "in arresting rebel depredations on

Usually assigned to deter smuggling, enforce custom laws, and assist stranded mariners, the U.S. Revenue Cutter Service also captured Confederate warships. Gil Cohen.

American commerce and transportation and in capturing rebels engaged therein."

Created in 1790 as the Revenue-Marine, the Cutter Service was formed following the American Revolutionary War. Weakened financially by years of strife, the United States struggled to stay afloat. Although much of the national income was derived from import levies, rampant smuggling cut much of the profits. The new organization took on the task of enforcing tariff and all other maritime laws. "They will endeavor to overcome difficulties," Treasury Secretary Alexander Hamilton wrote, "by a cool and temperate perseverance in their duty."

Vessels of the Revenue-Marine persevered through the Pirate Wars with France from 1798 to 1800, the War of 1812, and the Mexican-American War from 1846 to 1848. By 1832, revenue cutters had also begun conducting winter cruises to assist mariners, including those who were shipwrecked.

Cutter captains reported to and received their sailing orders from the Customs Collector at their assigned port. All crew pay, requests for supplies, arrangements for repairs, and mission assignments came directly from the port's Customs House. However, standing orders for individual cutters were stated in general terms, thus allowing captains to exercise their judgment and discretion.

Renamed in 1862, the Revenue Cutter Service merged with the Lifesaving Service in 1915 to form the U.S. Coast Guard. The Coast Guard also incorporated the U.S. Lighthouse Service in 1939 and the Navigation and Steamboat Inspection Service in 1942.

Sent to the Rescue

The night of January 10, 1862, found the *Elfin A. Kniper* struggling through high seas and a strong southwest gale. Although she was making good time, gusting winds crowded her toward shore. Unable to fight the storm any longer, the little schooner foundered at Half Moon Bay just a short distance from her final destination of San Francisco.

The storm wrecked havoc on the little town, too. According to a San Francisco newspaper, "From a gentleman who arrived from Half Moon Bay we learn that considerable damage was done at that place by the storm. A bridge was carried away and a man was drowned attempting to cross the creek. His boat capsized and he was carried out by the undertow."

The Revenue Cutter Shubrick *was dispatched to rescue the foundering* Elfin A. Kniper. U.S. Coast Guard.

The U.S. Revenue Cutter *Shubrick*, skippered by Capt. William C. Pease, was dispatched to the scene to rescue the crew and passengers. The *Shubrick*, a side-wheel steamer-brigantine, was a historic ship. Built in 1857 at the Philadelphia Navy Yard, she was the first steam-powered lighthouse tender and the first to be assigned to the West Coast.

Constructed of "Florida live oak and white oak," the vessel was 140 feet in length, 22 feet wide, and measured 339 tons. She was named for William Bradford Shubrick, a famous naval officer who served in the War of 1812 and in the Mexican-American War. In 1852, he was appointed the first chairman of the newly created Lighthouse Board.

The *Shubrick* was also the first lighthouse tender that was armed, carrying a twelve-pound gun and a twenty-four pound gun on a swivel carriage. "She was topped by a flush deck fore and aft. To better withstand buoys scraping her sides, the *Shubrick*'s hull was painted black, topped with a white ribbon and waist," reports noted. "Red paddle wheels, white paddle boxes, and a black bowsprit added a saucy touch to her long and graceful cutwater with six inches of bright copper shining above the waterline."

The cutter's maiden voyage to San Francisco was challenging. Running low on coal, the crew tore out the ship's hardwood paneling and broke up furniture for fuel. She also suffered from an outbreak of yellow fever which took the life of the assistant engineer. However, she successfully delivered the thirty-four remaining officers and crew along with one special passenger. He was Navy Commander J. DeCamp, who had been ordered to San Francisco as the first official inspector of California's Twelfth Lighthouse District.

The vessel spent the next three years setting buoys and carrying lighthouse supplies along the Pacific Coast. In 1859 she set the first buoys to mark the Columbia River. At the outbreak of the Civil War in 1861, she was ordered transferred to the control of the Revenue Cutter Service.

Ransacked

When the *Shubrick* steamed down from San Francisco to rescue the *Elfin A. Kniper*, she was also detailed to post a guard over the wreck to prevent looting of cargo upon which custom duties were due. Packaged in 200-pound sacks, only 8,000 of the 337,000 pounds of sugar remained. Capt. Pease was advised that most of it had been stolen by local residents.

Commander William B. Shubrick was the first chairman of the Lighthouse Board.
Author's collection.

"Half Moon Bay has lost reputation. When our Customs House officers went down in the steamer *Shubrick* to get the sugar that the captain of the schooner had saved, it couldn't be found," San Francisco newspapers snorted. "The Halfmooners rode down on fleet horses and galloped it all off. Some of it was traced to stores in town, but it had been emptied out of the bags into barrels to prevent identification."

Despite the sour grapes over the ransacked cargo, the *Shubrick* returned to San Francisco with the *Elfin A. Kniper*'s crew and "lady" passengers. Unhappily, the ship was reported a total loss. Within a few days of the wreck, the continuing gale battered the little schooner into kindling. It was a bittersweet ending to a successful career in the sugar trade.

Shubrick Epilogue

After the rescue, the *Shubrick* continued to perform customs and law enforcement duties under the command of Capt. Pease. She served the Cutter Service until 1866 when she was returned to the Lighthouse Board. On September 8, 1867, while transporting building material to the construction site of the Cape Mendocino lighthouse, the *Shubrick* ran aground in the fog. Thought to be a total loss, she was abandoned but her chief engineer, Thomas Winship, was able to save her.

"She is laying low broadside on the beach. The vessel is not materially injured as is generally supposed," a local newspaper reported. "The principal injury is a hole stove through her bottom for some four feet in diameter. The machinery is all removed to the beach above high tides."

With the help of a tug, the *Shubrick* was safely launched from the beach on June 20, 1868. The vessel proceeded to the San Francisco Navy Yard where she was rebuilt at a cost of over $162,000. Placed back in service in 1869, she remained active until 1885 when she was decommissioned and sold at Astoria, Oregon. Sadly, the *Shubrick*'s new owner was only interested in her copper and metal fittings. After running her aground, he stripped her of usable material and burnt her hull to salvage the fastenings.

3

FLOATING PALACE

NOVEMBER 8, 1868

The *Colorado* made history when she opened the portal of regular steamship service between California and the Orient. She also left an indelible mark on the perilous reefs of Point Montara.

Highest Seagoing Qualities

Built in 1865 by William H. Webb of New York, the passenger steamer *Colorado* was launched just before the end of the Civil War. At the time, there was still apprehension about roving Confederate warships. Although the *Colorado*'s speed was probably as much defense as she needed against potential raiders, the 3,728 ton vessel was armed with two twenty-pound and two thirty-pound guns. Included in her abundant arsenal were Sharp's rifles, muskets, revolvers, pikes, and axes. Travelers were reassured that, "The ship's crew of 120 men may be armed and marshaled on the hurricane deck in two minutes notice."

Webb was one of the most versatile and successful shipbuilders of his day. Born in New York in 1816, he built his first boat at the age of twelve and became apprenticed in his father's shipyard, Webb & Allen.

As a young man, he ventured off to Europe to learn more of foreign shipbuilding practices, particularly those of the shipyards in Scotland

and England. Unfortunately, his visit was cut short by the untimely death of his father at age forty-six in 1840. Just twenty-three years old, Webb assumed ownership of the near-bankrupt enterprise.

After settling his father's affairs and satisfying creditors, he reestablished the firm simply as William H. Webb. Between 1840 and 1869, he built 135 vessels, including packets, clippers, side-wheelers, ironclad warships, and steamships, creating more tonnage than any other American shipbuilder. Innovative and varied in his designs, Webb became known as "the very first naval architect in this country."

In addition to the *Colorado*, other prominent vessels Webb built were the *Challenge*, the first three-deck clipper ship; the *Cherokee*, the first steamship to run between New York and Savannah; the *California*, the first steamer to enter San Francisco's Golden Gate; and the USS *Dunderberg*, which never saw battle but was the largest of the Civil War iron-clad ships.

He closed his shipyard in 1869 to devote an increasingly greater amount of time to civic affairs. Described as "modest in demeanor and reserved in manner, with shrewd, intelligent eyes," Webb served as Chairman of the New York City Council on Political Reform, was a member of the Chamber of Commerce, and joined other industry leaders to found the Society of Naval Architects and Marine Engineers.

His most enduring legacy, however, was the founding of the Webb Academy and Home for Shipbuilders in 1889. The charter declared that the object of the thirteen acre site was "to afford gratuitous aid, relief and support to the aged, decrepit, invalid, indigent, or unfortunate men who have been engaged in building ships and to furnish to any young man of good character free education in the profession of shipbuilding."

Now known as the Webb Institute of Naval Architecture and Marine Engineering, the prestigious institute continues to offer a fully-accredited engineering program in naval architecture tuition-free.

Webb died at age eighty-three in 1899. Colleagues remembered him as a man with "a high order of genius. In all the vessels designed by him, great speed was combined with highest seagoing qualities, extraordinary carrying capacity, and the highest attainable strength. His shipyards were long the center of a marvelous industry, and his influence is still felt in the marine interests of this country."

Splendid Accommodations

In designing the *Colorado* for the Pacific Mail Steamship Company's Panama route, Webb produced the largest liner to ever ply the Pacific. The million dollar wooden side-wheel steamer boasted three decks, three masts, a round stern, and a length of 314 feet.

Hailed by the press as a "floating palace," she had fifty-two commodious staterooms on the main deck and 1,500 berths in steerage. A Pacific Mail advertisement bragged, "She has splendid accommodations for all class of passengers and large capacity for freight."

Founded in 1848 by the bold and energetic William Henry Aspinwall, Pacific Mail Steamship Company was an esteemed shipping line for over seventy-five years. The operating center was in San Francisco with corporate headquarters in New York. With the growing travel demands of California gold seekers, the firm began service between Panama and San Francisco in 1849. Tickets from New York to California ranged from $400 in first class to $125 in steerage.

The Panama route was a "short-cut" which eliminated the lengthy voyage around Cape Horn in South America. It became a vital link, carrying passengers and mail between the eastern United States and California. Hundreds of prospectors sailed from Atlantic ports, made a fifty-mile journey across the Isthmus by wagon, on mules, and on foot along jungle trails, and then took another ship for California. Although the trip remained strenuous, the Panama route shortened the voyage between New York and San Francisco from 15,000 to less than 6,000 miles.

"They have made arrangements for forwarding Bullion and Gold Dust confided to their care for transit across the Isthmus," one announcement said. "Coin and Gold dust should be put up in bags, and the bags carefully packed in boxes. Packages should not exceed in weight 125 lbs."

In 1855, Aspinwall completed construction of a railroad across Panama, offering the first service of its kind between the Atlantic and Pacific sides of the Isthmus. "He was a man of vision and courage," one historian wrote later of Aspinwall's accomplishments. "Where small men could only see the probability of the moment, he could grasp the possibility of the future."

Launched just before the end of the Civil War, the Colorado *carried armament against potential Confederate raiders.* San Francisco Maritime National Historical Park.

William H. Aspinwall founded the Pacific Mail Steamship Company in 1848. His vessels became a vital shipping link, carrying passengers and mail via the Panama route rather than around Cape Horn. Author's collection.

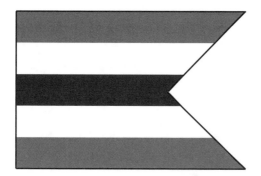

The house flag of Pacific Mail Line was a burgee, or swallowtail, red at top and bottom, blue in the center and white in between. Publisher's collection.

Coordination of rail and steamship schedules resulted in a remarkable travel time of twenty-one days between New York and San Francisco. As a result of its strong reputation for efficiency, dependability, and service, Pacific Mail flourished bringing an annual return on investment as high as thirty percent. The company became one of the most profitable enterprises of its era as well as an important part of the history of the American West.

Far East Pioneer

After being opened to the public for five days, the *Colorado* entered the water for the first time on April 1, 1865. Under the command of Capt. George H. Bradbury, she sailed from New York to San Francisco via Rio de Janeiro in Brazil, Callao on the coast of Peru, and Panama.

The following year, Congress awarded the Pacific Mail Steamship Company a $500,000 mail subsidy to make twelve round trips a year between San Francisco and Hong Kong via Yokohama, Japan. Prior to this, steam navigation in the Pacific had been confined to coastal routes in both the Americas and Asia.

Aspinwall lost no time in selecting the *Colorado* as the first American liner to carry mail across the Pacific to the Orient. In anticipation of the 6,340 mile journey, the vessel was refitted slightly. To improve her stability and increase her range, some steerage cabins and water tanks were removed and a fourth mast was added.

In 1867, Pacific Mail began the first regular steamship service across the Pacific Ocean. The *Colorado*'s inaugural voyage was highly anticipated. "At noon tomorrow, the red paddle wheels of the steamship Colorado will splash into San Francisco Bay on the Pacific Mail's first voyage to China. The craft's black wooden hull and brass are shined up for the occasion," the local press reported. "Tonight, 250 businessmen

The Colorado *opened the gateway to the Orient when the Pacific Mail Line received a subsidy to make trips from San Francisco.* Author's collection.

and dignitaries, including three Chinese merchants, attended the 'Grand China Mail Dinner' presided over by Governor Frederick F. Low."

Amid considerable fanfare on New Year's Day, 1867, the *Colorado* departed San Francisco with Capt. Bradbury at the helm. "That day was a great day for San Francisco, it seemed as if half the population was at hand to witness the sailing, which was to be the first steamboat to leave these shores for the faraway land across the Pacific," one report noted.

"Flags waved and bands played the national air. When the moment for the steaming arrived, the great side wheels churned the water and she backed away from the wharf. The crowds cheered wildly and the bands fluted to the high notes. Salutes were fired from guns on the steamer and on the wharves. One of the guns exploded and several people were hurt as we swung into the stream," the account continued.

"All the way down the bay the *Colorado* was saluted until we struck the open mouth of the sea. There were 150 passengers, every stateroom was taken and it was considered something of an honor to be a passenger on the first steamer to leave the Golden Gate for China."

Three weeks later, she arrived at Yokohama, and eight days later, on January 30th, she was at Hong Kong. The newspapers that she carried were newer by two weeks than those brought via the Mediterranean and Red Sea. Returning eastbound, the *Colorado* embarked the entire Japanese embassy, then en route to Washington.

A Shock

Unfortunately, after such a stellar beginning, the *Colorado* encountered troubles on a subsequent voyage. On November 9, 1868, carrying hundreds of passengers and the U.S. mail, the vessel ran aground on unseen shoals off Point Montara.

The steamer smacked onto the reef abruptly, alarming the passengers and creating a momentary panic aboard ship. Some of the unsuspecting travelers speculated that the shock was caused by a submarine earthquake. Others attributed the impact to a heavy sea which struck the ship, causing her to tremble.

"It was reported that she was well off shore in deep water and that the accident was unaccountable," newspapers commented. "It is now stated that Capt. Lapidge gave the ship into the hands of the first officer, who changed the course and ran her too near the shore, striking upon the bottom."

Bustling Hong Kong Harbor as it was during the 1860s. Author's collection.

Although the ship eventually floated free and all the passengers and mail survived, the near disaster left its mark on public sentiment. The ledge where the mishap occurred became known as Colorado Reef.

Taken to Hunter's Point, San Francisco where the dry dock was over 1,000 feet long, the *Colorado*'s hull was examined thoroughly. "An examination today showed that a hole had been broken through her bottom, on the port side, about twenty feet forward of her wheel, through which several fingers of a man's hands could be thrust," inspectors reported, "while the copper was ripped off a distance of ten feet, and the planking badly torn."

"From the splinters were taken several pieces of rock, which indicated that the ship must have struck upon a bottom of either soft or loose broken rock. Two new planks, about ten feet length, will make her bottom good as new. The copper was generally in a good condition, and only torn in a few places," the report continued. "This will be repaired and the ship will be able to make half-a-dozen trips to Panama and back before she is again docked. At least one hundred and ten thousand miles of running is expected before a ship demands new copper."

Unceremonious End

Meanwhile, Pacific Mail had constructed a quartet of new steamers specifically for the San Francisco to Hong Kong route. The four ships, the *China, Japan, Great Republic*, and *America*, were the largest and last of the great side-wheelers. In 1873 the first iron screw steamer entered the trade and by 1879 the life of these trans-Pacific side-wheelers was over.

When the *Great Republic* departed for the Far East on September 3, 1867, Pacific Mail announced sailings every six weeks. After the *Japan* entered service in August 1868, the company no longer needed the *Colorado* to maintain the schedule. Upon completion of her repairs, the *Colorado* returned to the San Francisco to Panama route.

Although the *Colorado* spent the next ten years mainly in the coastal work for which she was built, the steamer was kept as a "spare" ship to replace any of the other vessels when they were temporarily out of commission. She made a few more transpacific runs, several of which proved quite problematic.

On August 13, 1874 the *Colorado* was delayed in San Francisco by a crew strike yet still managed to transport 400 passengers, 900 tons of freight, and $338,000 in cargo to China. In 1875, she experienced difficulty when a severe storm in the mid-Pacific drove her far south of her course. The steamer made for Honolulu for coal and minor repairs but arrived in San Francisco in time to avoid concern.

Soon after leaving Hong Kong on another voyage in 1876, four of the 800 Chinese immigrants aboard the *Colorado* fell ill with small-pox and were left in the hospital at Yokohama. Not wanting to risk an epidemic when the ship arrived in San Francisco, the city's Quarantine Officer insisted that the steamer anchor off Mission Bay, just south of the primary port of entry. Passengers were unloaded cautiously, after which the vessel was inspected and fumigated.

In 1878, Pacific Mail began to modernize its aging fleet. Having paved the way for a rapid expansion of trade between California and the Far East, the *Colorado* was taken out of service. Sadly, the once stately steamer was sold for scrap the following year, bringing a unique chapter of maritime history to an unceremonious end.

After the Colorado *struck a reef at Point Montara, she was repaired and sailed on for another decade.* San Francisco Maritime National Historical Park.

4

MERSEY-MADE

OCTOBER 17, 1872

The loss of the British iron sailing ship *Aculeo* was engraved
in the memories of those who lived near Point Montara. The
wreck was so unforgettable that a fog signal was established to
warn other ships.

International Seaport

Once a small port tucked along the north bank of the muddy Mersey
River, Liverpool, England sprouted into an international seaport. With
the river stretching seventy miles through northwest England to greet
the Irish Sea, Liverpool was an ideal location for sending supplies to
Ireland and reaching other centers of commerce.

Originally, ships were simply tied up on the shoreline. As the port
grew busier, a dock was constructed in 1715 and others were added later.
Liverpool grew to be the third largest port in the country behind London
and Bristol. "Liverpool has an opulent, flourishing, and increasing trade
to Virginia and English colonies in America," writer Daniel Defoe
declared. "They trade round the whole island of Great Britain, send
ships to Norway, to Hamburg, and to the Baltic, and also to Holland and
Flanders (Belgium)."

By the 1800s, ships and shipyards dotted the waterfront at Liverpool, England which had sprouted into an international seaport. Author's collection.

In the 1800s, shipyards dotted the waterfront. One of the premiere shipbuilders of the day was Thomas B. Royden. Having been born into a working class family in the tiny village of Frankby, young Royden apprenticed in his father's carpentry trade. When his father retired, he moved to Liverpool. "Liverpool was a tempting place for tradesmen at the turn of the century with the port developing at an astonishing rate," one observer commented. "Dreams of wealth and prosperity beckoned many to seek their fortune."

Moving to Liverpool was a decision that would change his life. After securing employment as a master carpenter with Charles Grayson, a prominent shipbuilding firm, Royden opened his own yard in 1818. The enterprise, known as Thomas B. Royden & Company, began as a partnership with timber merchant Thomas Bland. Initially, the firm built small sailing ships. By 1854 they were producing iron-hulled sailing ships, and later steamships, for customers around the world.

One of those customers was David Duncan, who ordered the iron ship *Aculeo* in 1868 for his merchant shipping and trade ventures. Duncan was a former partner in Balfour, Williamson & Company, a prosperous South American trading firm with offices in Liverpool and Valparaiso, Chile. While they "were quite adventuresome in their business deals," the partnership ran into personal difficulties. Duncan returned to Liverpool around 1858 and continued his own business, Duncan, Fox & Company.

Duncan's business thrived with subsidiary offices in towns across Chile and Peru. He also had the pleasure of being greatly honored in public life, serving as a Director of the Royal Insurance Company and a Justice of the Peace. In 1885, he was elected as a Member of Parliament, a position he held until his death the following year.

Into the Fogs

While Duncan's life was long and full, the *Aculeo*'s was not. The vessel made several successful odysseys carrying general merchandise from England to South America and to the United States before disaster struck. Constructed of iron "with heavier plating than required," the vessel was 187 feet long, thirty-two feet wide, and measured 756 tons. On her final voyage, she was laden with a cargo of grain, 350 tons of pig and sheet iron, 100 tons of iron wire, 100 tons of coal, 150,000 yards of dry goods, 10,000 yards of linens, 50 tons of steel, and a wide variety of Christmas toys.

Thomas B. Royden, who built the Aculeo *in 1868, was one of the premiere ship-builders of the day.* Mike Royden.

Traveling via Montevideo, the capital and chief port of Uruguay, the *Aculeo* left Liverpool on April 1, 1872. Two hundred days later, the vessel was a mere twenty miles from her port of destination, San Francisco, when she encountered dense fog. Groping along the shrouded coast, Capt. T. McKay had nothing to guide him in his reckonings. "She had a fine passage," one newspaper observed, "until she got into the fogs which resulted in her destruction."

At 6:00 A.M. on October 17, 1872, the ship crashed to a sudden halt and lay impaled on the perilous rock formation called Colorado Reef. In moments, the vessel cracked open and filled with saltwater. In two hours, water engulfed the upper deck. The foggy coast off Point Montara had claimed another victim.

Capt. McKay and four of his crew left the ship, braving the breakers in a small boat. Time and time again, they fought the stinging surf. After several failed attempts, they landed ashore. Gradually, the exhausted group made their way to San Francisco while sixteen of the crew remained aboard the wreck. "It was not long, however, before the sea got up so high that they were afraid to stay by her and the seamen took to the boats," one account explained. "The sea broke over the ship and threatened to stave her to pieces every minute. After being in their boat twenty-four hours, they finally made shore."

Once in San Francisco, Capt. McKay reported to Cross & Company, his consignees, who dispatched the tug *Wizard* and the schooner *Sea Nymph* to the scene. However, salvage efforts were sluggish. "No active steps appear to be taken towards the recovery," one source commented. "The San Francisco purchasers seemed to be slow and apathetic in their movements, and it is reported that considerable discontent and disagreement exists among the wrecking company."

The delay proved costly. As the salvagers arrived, a heavy gale broke upon the scene, shattering the ship and sweeping most of the $150,000 cargo out to sea. Rigging, spars, and smashed boxes of toys littered the beach.

What was left of the *Aculeo* lay on a sharp jutting reef three miles from the beach. Her masts remained standing but a portion of her wooden bulwarks had been ripped apart by the angry surf. A local newspaper described the carnage: "Her rattlin' shrouds all steeped in foam, with her masts went by the board, like a vessel of glass she stove and sunk, Ho! Ho! the breakers roared."

Sadly, even an iron ship could not withstand such a terrible beating. A total loss, the remains of the *Aculeo* slipped slowly beneath the waves and sank from sight.

Although the *Aculeo* was lost, some of the Christmas toys survived. According to one account, "Captain McKay salvaged a china doll and slipped it into the arms of the first little girl he saw."

Something of a Castaway

For years, the wreck was etched into the memory of many residents and was even immortalized by a local artist. Known as the "Dean of San Mateo coastal artists," Galen Wolf captured the scene in a work called "The Toy Ship." The rendering is one of sixteen pieces that are part of his noted series called *Legends of the Coastland.* He wrote stories to accompany the paintings.

Born in San Francisco in 1889, Galen Russell Wolf grew up with three brothers in Victorian wealth. His father, an enterprising young businessman, built a booming import-export company trading with the Far East. The family home faced the harbor and sailing ships could be seen easily. "Galen remembered them arriving with broken spars and masts, loose rigging, and cracked hulls," Shannon Nottestad, who is preparing the *Legends* for publication, revealed. "Sea captains were often dinner guests at the Wolf mansion, and young Galen listened avidly as they spoke of the sea and foreign lands."

On weekends, the family traveled south by wagon to visit relatives along the San Mateo coast. Wolf stayed happily absorbed in adventurous yarns spun by his grandfather, a veteran seaman who journeyed around Cape Horn in a clipper ship. Wandering the beaches together, they watched eagerly for passing sailing vessels and scouted for remnants of wrecked ships.

At the age of fourteen, Wolf entered the San Francisco studio of Gertrude Boyle, a free-spirited artist who introduced him to well known literary and artistic figures of the times. Finding himself in the company of environmentalist John Muir, writer Jack London, landscape artist William Keith, and others, Wolf discovered a new creative universe. He was inspired further by French impressionists when he spent a year in Europe studying art.

Then, on the morning of April 18, 1906, two sharp tremors rattled San Francisco and its surrounding areas. The entire city was relentlessly shaken and twisted. Ships at dockside shuddered and shook. Untold

Coastal artist Galen Wolf, who captured the wreck of the Aculeo *on canvas, had a special connection to the ship.* Author's collection/Marvin & Ressa Fairbanks.

numbers of lives, homes, and treasured items were lost, including most of young Galen's paintings. Thoroughly distraught, Wolf turned his interests elsewhere. He fished, hiked through the Sierras, and spent twenty years farming and raising a family in the Sacramento Delta. Feeling a bit of a castaway, he left his family in 1932 to return to the simplicity and serenity of coastal life.

Wolf took up the brush again, selling his paintings for $4 to $5 apiece and conducting art classes on local beaches. "He loved living on the coast," Wolf's daughter, Ressa Fairbanks admitted. "He roamed the coastside painting on anything he could get his hands on — canvas, paper, cardboard, plywood."

About 1950, Wolf began work on *Legends of the Coastland*. The series depicts dramatic scenes of coastal life in the 1800s within a highly stylized watercolor mosaic which was his invention. Wolf's innovative approach was nothing short of amazing. By that time, cataracts had claimed most of his vision.

In the *Legends*, Wolf brings to life his grandfather's tales of sailing ships and voyages gone awry. "The Toy Ship," which depicts the wreck of the *Aculeo*, held special significance. In it, Wolf depicts a doll drifting underwater, awaiting rescue. He knew that her voyage was not over, that she would be saved, but that she would be lost in San Francisco's 1906 earthquake. He knew because the little girl Capt. McKay had given the doll was Wolf's mother.

A Dangerous Locality

The wreck of the *Aculeo* made a lasting impression on others, as well. "Only a fortnight ago, we directed the attention of lighthouse engineers to the absolute necessity for a fog whistle. Had this been erected, this accident would never have occurred," the *San Mateo County Gazette* noted indignantly. "It is to be hoped no more time or vessels will be lost ere steps be taken to have provided these accommodations. The value of an *Aculeo* or two, would be sufficient to erect all the safety appliances requisite for this coast."

In March of 1873, Congress appropriated $15,000 for a fog signal at Point Montara, to be positioned at the end of a rocky bluff seventy feet above the ocean. According to the *Coast Pilot*, the bluff "terminates in cliffs with numerous outlying rocks … a dangerous locality in thick weather."

Galen Wolf's rendering, "The Toy Ship," portrays the Aculeo's *tragic final voyage.*
Allen Bunes & Shannon Nottestad.

For early mariners sailing close to the coast as they approached the Golden Gate, this particular patch of "thick weather" was especially hazardous. At the time, officials thought a fog signal would be more useful than a lighthouse for navigating through the area's murky mist.

On March 1, 1875, a twelve-inch steam whistle, similar to whistles used on ships and locomotives, began operation at Point Montara as the third fog signal station (with no light tower) established in California. Earlier fog signals were positioned to the south in 1872 at Año Nuevo Island and in 1874 at Yerba Buena Island inside San Francisco Bay.

At the same time, a Victorian duplex, which still stands, was constructed on the exposed, isolated bluff above Colorado Reef. The quarters housed two keepers and their families. The first head keeper was Henry Thomas Holbrook who moved on to Pigeon Point Lighthouse in 1878. His salary was a mere $1,000 per year. Keeper Holbrook also served at other California lighthouses, including Cape Mendocino and Point Arena. Later, he became a private detective. According to Robert Hanssen, Holbrook's great-great-grandson, "He was a handsome man, sort of a ladies' man, and something of a scalawag," Hanssen exclaimed. "Apparently, he ran afoul of the law on more than one occasion."

Despite the challenging weather, the men kept the fog signal mechanism functioning in good order. Fog could last for days, requiring them to constantly stoke the boilers and tend the signal. Point Montara was often fog-bound forty or more days each year.

Running the installation proved costly, too. Energy to operate the fog signal came from steam pressure created by heating water with a coal fire. Between 150,000 and 200,000 pounds of coal a year were needed to fuel the boiler for the twelve-inch whistle. Often, the boiler took up to forty-five minutes to develop enough steam pressure to operate the fog signal.

A hydraulic ram forced water from nearby Montara Creek to the fog signal building and its 2,000 gallon reservoir. A hydraulic ram is a water pump in which the downward flow of naturally running water is intermittently halted by a valve so that the flow is forced upward through an open pipe into a reservoir. The old ram face is still visible on the creek from the cove beneath the lighthouse.

Every thirty seconds, the fog-piercing, five-second blast could be heard from as far as fifteen miles out at sea. Unfortunately, the fog signal was not enough to prevent continuing disasters surrounding the treacherous ledges of Colorado Reef.

In 1875, three years after the wreck of the Aculeo, *a fog signal was established at Point Montara.* Christopher Bauman.

Although nine lighthouses were constructed in California by 1872, including a new one at Pigeon Point twenty-eight miles south of Point Montara and one to the north at Fort Point at the entrance to the Golden Gate, a light would not be established at Point Montara until 1900. By then, other hapless vessels would meet tragic ends.

5

A GRAVE ERROR

OCTOBER 17, 1876

F our years to the day that the *Aculeo* was impaled on Colorado Reef, the three-masted British vessel *Rydal Hall* crashed in the same vicinity. The ship, the cargo, and ten of the ship's crew perished.

Cardiff Coal

In the otherwise pastoral valleys of South Wales, Great Britain, it was the iron industry that caused the tiny town of Cardiff to evolve as a port. Initially, the demand for iron was fueled by the Royal Navy, which needed iron cannons for its ships, and later by the construction of new railroads needing iron rails.

In 1794, a canal was completed linking Cardiff with Merthyr. Located just north of Cardiff, Merthyr was situated close to vast reserves of iron ore, coal, limestone, and water, making it an ideal site for ironworks. In 1798, a basin was created, connecting the canal to the sea. Cardiff's first dock was built in 1839 and two years later a railway opened, igniting the city's growth.

"The inhabitants of this town carry on considerable trade and send thither great quantities of oats, barley, salt butter, and poultry of all kinds," a writer noted. "There are not less than 8,780 tons of cast iron and wrought iron shipped annually to London and other places."

In the 1850s, coal quickly replaced iron as the industrial foundation of South Wales. A reliable energy source for hundreds of years, coal was an important fuel for cities, industries, railroads, and steamships. With yearly exports reaching two million tons as early as 1862, Cardiff coal was to that era what oil is today.

Originally, coal was brought down from the hills and valleys on the backs of mules. Their burden was laid down at a small quay, loaded on small vessels and carried to other ports. By 1870, with its burgeoning docks and railways, larger ships could be accommodated and Cardiff was providing thirty percent of Britain's coal exports. "The scene on the wharves is very stirring," an observer wrote. "There is a network of railways about the docks, giving direct communication to every port in the kingdom."

Fat Cargo Carrier

Ships such as the *Rydal Hall* were used as colliers to transport coal from Cardiff, not only to British ports, but to ports around the world. Built in 1874 at Liverpool, England by Robert Alexander, the 1,771 ton vessel served as both a cargo and passenger ship, providing service to America, Australia, and India.

Born in Belfast, Ireland, Alexander was a distinguished shipbroker who established the Sun Shipping Company in 1868. With Alexander's penchant for naming his ships "Hall" after notable people and places in Britain, the enterprise was known popularly as the Hall Line. Indeed, it was his hallmark. However, it wasn't until 1899 that the company name was officially changed to Hall Line Ltd.

The Hall Line house flag was blue on the right and left quadrants and lettering, and white in the top and bottom quadrants. Publisher's collection.

Bound for San Francisco, the *Rydal Hall* departed Cardiff on June 23, 1876 under the command of Capt. Henry Foster. Over 260 feet long and forty-two feet wide, the iron vessel was a "fat cargo carrier which could match anybody else's hulls for capacity." In addition to a crew of thirty-three, she carried 2,551 tons of coal consigned for Balfour, Guthrie, & Company.

Balfour, Guthrie & Company was associated with the eminent British firm of Balfour, Williamson & Company. Established by three Scotsmen in 1851, Balfour, Williamson & Company began as a meager merchant shipping and South American trade enterprise and grew into a "first-class Liverpool house."

Alexander Balfour ran the Liverpool operation while his two partners, Stephen Williamson and David Duncan, worked in Valparaiso, Chile. After a falling out with Balfour, Duncan left the partnership to begin his own company. One of the ships he built was the *Aculeo* which wrecked near Point Montara in 1872.

On a voyage to Chile in 1864, Balfour experienced the difficult conditions sailors endured, especially rounding the infamous Cape Horn. "Wet to the skin, the crew spent hours clinging to the yardarms. Because of the danger of fire, no drying facilities or fires were allowed," one account said. "At this point in the journey, fresh food had usually run out. This resulted in many of the crew suffering from poor health that often led to a premature death."

When he returned to Liverpool, Balfour founded the Duke Street Home to provide better conditions for sailors. He was also a founder of orphanages for seamen's children as well as the Seamen's Institute. When Balfour died in 1886, a monument was erected in his memory on the grounds of St. John's Gardens in Liverpool. The inscription reads, "His life was devoted to God in noble and munificent efforts for the benefit of sailors, the education of people, and the promotion of all good works."

Having acquired considerable experience trading from Chile with large, efficient sailing ships, the trio expanded operations to San Francisco in 1869 by establishing Balfour, Guthrie & Company. Initially, the firm imported British industrial goods and exported wheat from California. They soon established the largest grain-export and fruit-packing venture in the West. Alexander Balfour's brother, Robert, and Alexander Guthrie were principal officers of the firm.

In 1876, Balfour, Guthrie & Company opened an office in Portland, Oregon followed by one in Tacoma in 1888. Other branches of Balfour,

Balfour,
Guthrie & Co.

SHIPPING AND COMMISSION MERCHANTS

SEATTLE, WASH.

San Francisco   Portland   Tacoma

Importers of   Exporters of
CEMENT, PIG IRON   WHEAT
FIRE BRICK   FLOUR
FIRE CLAY   LUMBER
PIG TIN and   and
CHEMICALS   SALMON

SELLING AGENTS
for
THE AMERICAN TINPLATE CO.

VIEWS OF THE BALFOUR DOCK. TACOMA

When the Rydal Hall *went aground in 1876, she carried a cargo of coal consigned to the prominent firm of Balfour, Guthrie & Company.* University of Washington Libraries.

Williamson & Company were established worldwide well into the 1900s.

Terrible Night

The *Rydal Hall*'s long journey proved typically uneventful until the evening of October 17th. Running along with a light breeze and in thick fog, Capt. Foster believed his ship to be twenty miles from the Farallon Lighthouse. Located on one of the islets forming the rugged Farallon Islands twenty-three miles west of San Francisco Bay, the tower was the third lighthouse established in California.

Unable to take readings as the fog thickened, he gave the order to "heave to." This is a way of slowing the ship's forward progress by fixing the helm and foresail position so that the vessel doesn't have to be actively steered. This tactic was commonly used while waiting out a storm or other bad weather.

"As the night wore on it grew thicker and thicker, and we grew a little nervous. All the officers and myself remained on deck and were on deck when she struck," Capt. Foster stated later. "I did not hear any fog whistle nor had I any idea where we were. She did not strike hard, but it appeared as if her bottom was crushed, and she rapidly filled with water."

Panic-stricken, four of the crew, George Johns, George Geoger, George White, and Charles Wilson seized a small boat without the captain's orders, and lowered away. Unluckily, the boat swamped in the heavy surf and all were drowned.

Moments later, the captain ordered a lifeboat to be cleared away, putting Second Mate Hugh Williams in charge. After considerable confusion, eight men including Williams, seamen William Baker, Alexander Barlow, and James Gomez, steward Fred Davis and steward's boy William Wilson, and apprentices C. Clayton and Keith Selwyn, scrambled aboard.

As the men struggled to lower the lifeboat, huge waves broke over the deck flinging the boat overboard. Everyone was catapulted into the churning water. Somehow, Clayton and Davis managed to swim to some rocks and cling to them until being plucked off by a band of courageous local fishermen. Sadly, the others, including Selwyn who was only sixteen years old, were swallowed by the sea.

Capt. Foster made no further attempts to lower other lifeboats. With little hope, he and the remaining crew stayed aboard the sinking ship until morning. Fortunately, vessels from a nearby whaling station arrived and with some difficulty rescued the bedraggled group. "We passed a terrible night on the wrecked ship," the captain declared, "the sea beating over her all night and the cold being almost insufferable."

Toward morning the tide receded, leaving the ship's decks almost clear. The *Rydal Hall* still hung firm on the rocks about an eighth of a mile from the shore. With her hold full of water and her hull breaking, the vessel's chances of surviving was gone. One observer reflected, "She was a fine iron ship."

As dawn broke, Francisco "Chico" Gonzales joined other local townspeople who gathered to scoop up coal washing onto the beach. It would provide free fuel for the coming winter months. Gonzales salvaged something else, too, a plain wooden sea chest bobbing in the surf. Through the years, the chest was passed on to others in the family.

"That old sea chest has been around since I was a little kid," Chico's great-grandson, John E. Gonzales, Jr., exclaimed. "My dad packed it around with him everywhere, in the Navy, and to all the lighthouses where he served." It was an appropriate memento, indeed, for John, Sr., who was Head Keeper at Point Montara Lighthouse from 1955 to 1963.

Aftermath

The rest of the *Rydal Hall*'s wreckage was auctioned by S.L. Jones & Co. on October 20th at the Merchants' Exchange in San Francisco and sold for $850 to Breeze and Loughran. "If we have fine weather," newspapers commented, "they will raise a good profit on their investment by saving spars, sails, rigging, anchors, chains, and provisions."

Unfortunately, the crippled ship languished on the rocks without a thing being done toward salvage. Apparently, some difficulty occurred between the purchasers and the men they hired to perform recovery efforts. Valued at $120,000, the ship and its cargo was a total loss.

Gradually, the *Rydal Hall* began breaking apart. Chunks of Cardiff coal, cabin fittings, and other debris spilled into the water and onto the beach. A large portion of the vessel's woodwork was sighted drifting past the Cliff House, a restaurant perched on a high pinnacle on the outskirts of San Francisco. Nothing was saved, not even the ship's papers.

Meanwhile, Silas Casey, Jr., the Lighthouse Inspector, investigated Capt. Foster's allegation that the fog signal was inaudible. Casey was

Washed ashore from the wreck of the Rydal Hall, *this weathered wooden sea chest has been in the family of Francisco "Chico" Gonzales for over 130 years.* Julie Barrow.

John E. Gonzales, Sr., later a keeper at the Point Montara Lighthouse, packed his Navy gear in a sea chest salvaged from the Rydal Hall *by his grandfather.* John E. Gonzales, Jr.

Auction Sales.

S. L. JONES & CO.,
AUCTIONEERS.

THIS DAY.

FRIDAY.................October 20, 1876

AT 1½ O'CLOCK P. M.,

At the Merchants' Exchange, California St.

WE WILL SELL

For account of whom it may concern,

By order of Captain M. H. Foster and
the Marine Surveyors,

THE BRITISH IRON SHIP

"Rydall Hall,"

Burthen per Register, 1864 Tons.

Together with all her

Furniture, Tackle, Apparel,

ETC., ETC., ETC.

As she now lies on the beach, abreast of
DENISTOWN RANCH, near the Whaling
Station, together with her entire cargo,
consisting of about

2551 tons best Cardiff Steam Coal.

Terms Cash in U. S. gold coin.

S. L. JONES & CO.,
o20   Auctioneers.

The wreck of the Rydal Hall *was sold at auction for $850. Little was saved before she sank.* Daily Alta California.

a respected naval officer and veteran of the Civil War. After graduating from the U.S. Naval Academy at Annapolis in 1860, he served aboard ships in both the Southern and Northern Blockading Squadrons. By 1876, when he was assigned to the Lighthouse Service, he had risen to the rank of Commander.

Commander Casey verified that local whaling crews could hear the whistle distinctly, and that on the night of the wreck, the wind had been blowing in a southerly direction. The log of the Point Montara fog station showed that the fog signal was running at an average of seventy pounds per square inch of steam which meant that it was heard within a radius of three miles. Casey concluded that since the ship went ashore about two-and-a-half miles from Point Montara — the crew had to have heard it.

Casey's conclusion only added to the troubles of the hapless captain who had been stumbling about in the fog. After a Naval Court hearing at the British Consulate in San Francisco, Capt. Foster was found guilty of a "grave error in judgment" and lost his master's certificate for a year.

Casey stayed on as Lighthouse Inspector until 1879, later serving at another lighthouse district. When he retired from the Navy in 1903, he had risen to the rank of Rear Admiral. He died in Warm Springs, Virginia ten years later.

Resurfacing

In 1877, diver James Steele descended upon the remains of the *Rydal Hall* and retrieved an anchor and a small amount of chain. In 1971, divers Roy Lee and John Koepf rediscovered the sunken hulk quite by accident while poking around the reef on an abalone hunt.

As expected, there wasn't much left. "The only thing that remains to shape the boat are a few iron ribs," Lee shrugged. "There are some plates lying around, too, and when we lift off those plates, we sometimes find artifacts underneath." Most of the artifacts were donated to the San Mateo County Historical Society, including a bronze porthole, the bronze scrollwork on the ladder leading to the captain's cabin, and a thirty pound iron ingot.

Working in murky, rough water, the divers also raised an enormous anchor, which is still on display in front of a Half Moon Bay seafood restaurant. It required three huge air buoys and a giant crane to lift the fourteen foot, two ton anchor out of fifteen feet of water. "The anchor was rusty orange and rubbed clean on its top," newspapers reported, "but on the bottom, it was encrusted with seaweed, barnacles, one star fish, and a small abalone."

In 1972, Lee and Koepf located another anchor and a thousand pound, six-foot deck cannon. They struggled for two hours, tugging and chaining the heavy cannon to four floating buoys made of old fifty-five gallon oil drums, before it was raised successfully. Raising this second anchor proved equally challenging.

Surprisingly, the two divers also recovered the ship's bell. Using a wrecking bar, they labored for four hours before prying the bell away from solidified coal and old ironwork. The duo spent several hours more chipping away at the salt-encrusted, hundred-pound, bronze bell before uncovering its identifying marks: "*Rydal Hall* – 1874."

"When I spotted a knob sticking up out of the pile, I knew it was something," Koepf exclaimed. "The bell is priceless."

After ninety-five years on the ocean floor, the ill-starred *Rydal Hall* had resurfaced after all.

In the early 1970s, divers discovered the sunken remains of the Rydal Hall. *They resurrected scores of artifacts, including this bronze, hundred-pound, ship's bell.* San Mateo County History Museum.

6

MEANT TO SAIL

SEPTEMBER 26, 1881

During her brief history, an illustrious line of master mariners and adventurous seafaring men stood upon the decks of the *Alice Buck*. Once a fading memory, her terrible fate was captured on canvas for all to see.

A Successful Ship

The *Alice Buck* was meant to sail forever. For good luck, she was named for a granddaughter of Jonathan Buck who founded Bucksport, one of Maine's earliest shipbuilding centers. For good measure, her future was put into the hands of several legendary sea captains.

The vessel first entered the water in 1870 at Belfast, Maine on Penobscot Bay. Built and owned by Capt. Henry McGilvery, the *Alice Buck* was 198 feet long, thirty-eight feet wide, and measured 1,425 tons. Coppering of the ship's hull was completed in England where such materials were cheaper.

Although the *Alice Buck* served briefly in the transatlantic cotton trade, the hardy ship spent most of her career shuttling goods to the Far East and to San Francisco. "While she has no fast voyages to her

Capt. Henry McGilvery, a noted shipmaster, built and owned the Alice Buck. *The vessel entered the water in 1870 at Belfast, Maine on Penobscot Bay.* Penobscot Marine Museum.

credit," one account declared, "she made good passages and was called a successful ship."

Raised in Stockton, Maine which lies at the head of Penobscot Bay, Capt. McGilvery started sea life as a boy. Rapidly rising from seaman to master, he commanded vessels in the lucrative China trade. He is said to have skippered the first American ship to enter Singapore harbor. In 1852, at the age of thirty-three, Capt. McGilvery retired to embark on shipbuilding ventures in Stockton. Six years later, he moved on to Belfast where the waterfront was a hub of commercial activity.

Later, he made his home in nearby Hallowell on the banks of the Kennebec River. Capt. McGilvery died in 1890 at the age of seventy-one while visiting a daughter in Brooklyn, New York. "He was a man of high character and of remarkable ability," a biographer noted, "both as a shipmaster and a businessman."

Master of Fine Ships

Capt. McGilvery's choice to command the *Alice Buck* was Capt. Phineas Pendleton II, of Searsport, Maine. Located just north of Belfast, Searsport was known as "the home of the famous sea captains." During the 1870s and 1880s, the port's seventeen shipyards built two hundred ships and supplied over ten percent of the nation's merchant marine deep water captains.

Capt. Pendleton went to sea at age sixteen as a cook and went on to command more than thirty different vessels. Over the years, he became wealthy through successful management of his shipping property and was dubbed a "master and builder of some of the finest ships that sailed the ocean." During the Civil War, he met with large losses at the hands of plundering Confederate privateers. Despite the setback, he made repeated visits to Washington, D.C. and ultimately received due compensation.

A kind-hearted and generous man, Capt. Pendleton was renowned for maintaining a productive crew and for taking his vessels safely to port. "A fair illustration to show his kindness," one story goes, "is that he hove his ship to in mid ocean when he was making eight knots an hour at twelve o'clock at night to pick up a monkey that a vicious boy threw overboard."

On land, he was equally regarded for his good nature and was often called, "Uncle Phineas." A friend commented, "His hearty and genial

Capt. Phineas Pendleton II was the first of an illustrious line of sea captains to command the Alice Buck. *Penobscot Marine Museum.*

manners, storytelling capacity and extended experiences in all parts of the world made him a most entertaining companion."

Capt. Pendleton died in 1895 at the age of eighty-nine. "He was a man of striking appearance and many qualities united in making him a profitable friend and acquaintance," an obituary said. "Maine loses one of its old time sea captains of much business capacity and a prominent and highly respected citizen."

Innovative Commander

After only a handful of voyages aboard the *Alice Buck*, Capt. Pendleton turned the helm over to his son-in-law. Capt. William H. Blanchard had a fine reputation, too, and was innovative when a ship was in trouble.

On a previous vessel, a rudder and steering post were lost in a gale while rounding deadly Cape Horn. "Capt. Blanchard hove to, set his crew to work, jury-rigged a rudder and improvised a steering gear," one report asserted. "Then, he sailed around the Horn with this rig, made stops to unload and load cargo at several West Coast ports, and then sailed back to New York on his homemade rudder and steering gear."

He was also a handy man to have around when a doctor was needed. While harbored in Kobe, Japan during a typhoon, Capt. Blanchard noticed distress signals coming from a bark he owned, the *Willard Mudgett*. He learned that Mrs. Dickie, the captain's wife, needed a physician for childbirth but no one could leave port in such a violent storm.

Capt. Blanchard offered his services and shortly presided over the birth of a baby girl. "Capt. Blanchard was experienced," a colleague boasted, "as he had officiated at the birth of five of his children on shipboard." The child became an actress of note, sharing the bill with performers such as James Stewart, Carole Lombard, Cesar Romero, and Judy Garland in the 1930s and 1940s. Using the stage named of Clara Blandic (Clara for Mrs. Blanchard, Blan for Capt. Blanchard, and Dic for her family name), she is best known as Auntie Em in "Wizard of Oz."

Unfortunately, Capt. Blanchard had his share of misfortunes as well as successes. While on a lengthy voyage from Boston to Valencia, Spain on the ship *Bosphorus*, his wife was taken ill and was left in Brazil to return to the United States. Upon arriving in Valencia, Capt. Blanchard went ashore to attend to business details. A sudden gale arose, tossing the *Bosphorus* ashore and shattering the ship and its cargo. All but five

Capt. William H. Blanchard was innovative when a ship was in trouble. Penob-scot Marine Museum.

of the crew drowned, including the first and second mates who were Capt. Blanchard's brothers, Edward and Locke.

On another vessel, he survived a fire at sea near Manila, and soon after retired from sea life. In 1904, Capt. Blanchard sailed as a passenger on the *Willard Mudgett*, the same ship upon which he had delivered a baby. On this voyage, the vessel was laden with coal and was commanded by his twenty-eight year old son, Capt. Frederick P. Blanchard. Known as "a good sailer," the ship foundered in a heavy northeast gale while bound from Norfolk, Virginia to Bangor, Maine. Neither the vessel nor anyone on board was seen or heard from again.

Anchors and Apricots

Following Capt. Blanchard in 1880 was Capt. James R. Herriman. The forty-three-year-old skipper hailed from an old seafaring family in Bangor, Maine which lies thirty miles up the Penobscot River. He had vast experience commanding barks, brigs, and other fill-rigged ships such as the *Alice Buck*.

His father, Hezekiah, also a native of Maine, was a respected ship master. Upon his father's death, James was taken by his mother to Prospect and then to Winterport where he attended school. Like other young adventure seekers, he was struck with "sea fever" at the age of fifteen and shipped out as a cabin boy. Herriman became captain of his first vessel at only twenty-two, engaging in merchant trade with the East Indies, Europe, and California.

During the Civil War, Capt. Herriman commanded a transport ship, conveying troops and heavy munitions for Union naval forces. He carried men, shot, and shell, to numerous strategic battle locations including the York River in Virginia and Annapolis Harbor in Maryland. Capt. Herriman was also among the Union throng that launched an assault on Fort Jackson and Fort St. Philip for the capture of New Orleans.

The largest city in the Confederacy, New Orleans was threatened by naval forces both to the north and to the south. Trusting that the two forts could thwart any attack from the south, the Confederacy put nearly all its efforts into defending the city to the north.

Meanwhile, the Union mounted a siege on the forts with 18,000 soldiers and a fleet of warships, mortar rafts, and support vessels. Rebel forces were obliterated, and the subsequent capture of New Orleans was a fatal blow from which the Confederacy never recovered.

Capt. James R. Herriman hailed from an old seafaring family.
Penobscot Marine Museum.

After his discharge in 1864, Capt. Herriman returned to his old trade in the mercantile business. When he retired from sea life, he was briefly engaged as a marine surveyor in San Francisco. Shortly thereafter, he purchased a ranch near Saratoga in California's fertile Santa Clara Valley, naming it "The Anchorage." The bountiful ranch had nearly twenty-three acres of apricots, cherries, peaches, and plums. In 1887, the first year of production, competitors observed enviously that "the ranch produced twelve tons of apricots and five tons of peaches, paying eight percent interest on the investment."

An Awful Crash

Filling in for Capt. Herriman on the *Alice Buck*'s last passage was Capt. Herman Henningsen. Bound for Portland, Oregon, with a cargo destined for the Northern Pacific Railroad, the *Alice Buck* departed New York on April 7, 1881. Building the new railroad, which was completed in 1883, was critical to opening the Pacific Northwest. The 1,780 ton payload, valued at over $100,000, consisted of 6,668 bars of railroad iron; 1,500 bundles of fishplates for joining or fixing rails; 299 kegs of bolts; 669 railway fasteners called dog spikes; and twenty-eight cases of furniture.

On August 28, 1881, the *Alice Buck* encountered a hurricane in the Pacific and sprang a leak in the bow. The following day, a second gale pelted the gurgling ship, pouring more water into the already saturated hold. Desperate, Capt. Henningsen steered for San Francisco in hope of repairs. The weary crew worked day and night at the pumps, but the leak only worsened.

At 4:00 P.M. on September 26th, the captain calculated the ship to be fifty-five miles southwest of the Golden Gate. On making the coast, not a breath of wind stirred the air. However, a "pretty good sea was running," forcing the *Alice Buck* toward the shores of Half Moon Bay. "Shortly after midnight, under clear and starry skies, the ship struck with an awful crash on the rocks about 1,500 feet from a high bluff," newspapers explained. "She bumped five or six times, bows-on, and at last hit hard and broke in two."

By now, the crew was exhausted and Capt. Henningsen had been on deck steadily for three days and nights. A dinghy was launched but upset almost immediately. Two men were washed ashore, one drowned. "That was the last seen of them," a grim-faced captain revealed later.

Another boat containing the two mates, the steward, and two seamen, was launched but smashed while being lowered. Two of the men scrambled aboard again. The rest disappeared beneath the churning surf. When there was not enough of the crumbling hull to cling to, Capt. Henningsen ordered the remaining crew to don life preservers and jump overboard. As one of the deckhouses floated by, the captain and fourteen-year-old cabin boy George Parker seized hold of it. Young Parker clambered aboard while the captain floated alongside. Moments later, four others swam over and climbed on, too.

"George asked me if I was afraid and I said no," Capt. Henningsen reflected. "He said, 'all right, as long as you keep up and along with me I'll be all right.' As they drifted off I sang out 'good-bye,' and he answered me cheerfully. Before they reached shore the undertow capsized them."

One of the capsized seamen snatched Parker from the surging swells and drifting debris. Unluckily, a heavy wave thrust a chunk of lumber against the lad, knocking him from the sailor's arms. The stout-hearted young cabin boy was swept away by the swirling surf.

The floating wreckage prevented Capt. Henningsen from making much headway. After drifting for nine hours in the freezing water, the captain and a handful of others were rescued by the cargo steamer *Salinas*. The 154-ton vessel, built by James Brennan of Watsonville, California to haul farm produce, household goods, and lime between Santa Cruz and San Francisco, was in the area by sheer chance.

Ashore, two nineteen-year-old farm boys, Silas Hovious and Frank Hale, heroically saved three of the ship's crew. Upon viewing the disastrous scene from the bluff tops, the duo shimmied down an eighty-foot cliff, shouted to those above to throw down a rope, and hauled the drowning men from the sea. "We just clumb along somehow. We didn't think much of how we were doing it," the boys mumbled shyly. "We only thought of that sailor in the water."

Sadly, nine of the *Alice Buck*'s crew of twenty drowned. Those lost were: first mate William Barry; second mate D. Crocker; cabin boy George Parker; seamen David Black, John Gunnison, Charles Reader, and Patrick Welch; the cook, and the steward.

Doomed and Deserted

The *Alice Buck* was a total loss. On October 12th, the famous Merritt Wrecking Company was dispatched to salvage the iron portion of the cargo. Flying its house flag showing a black stallion in full gallop, the firm was nicknamed "The Black Horse of the Sea." The ironic symbol played on the old term of "white horses," the name given by seafarers to waves breaking into foam.

Capt. Israel J. Merritt started the company in 1860 when salvage operations were in their infancy. With $50,000, he established offices on Wall Street in New York, San Francisco, and Norfolk, Virginia under the name of Coast Wrecking Company.

The 1850s and 1860s were a dangerous time for mariners and marine operations around the American continent. Along with the transition from sail to steam came unreliable equipment. The growing needs of commerce which fueled U.S. expansion also resulted in larger numbers of vessels plying the sea. Consequently, countless ships foundered, leaving companies like Merritt's to do the harrowing and uncertain work of salvage. "They were a rough-hewn, brash, and stoic group," one writer disclosed, "willing to pit themselves against the sea, their endeavors always high risk, and if fortune smiled, high gain."

Over the years, Coast Wrecking Company saved hundreds of valuable vessels and cargoes, amounting to millions of dollars. The company was known and respected as a pioneer and a leader in the field. "As submarine engineers, divers, and wreckers, these gentlemen have no equal on this continent," admirers maintained. "They own a fleet of steamers, sailing vessels, and pontoons specially built for this work, seaworthy in all weathers, and rigged and fitted regardless of cost."

In 1880, Merritt's son, Israel, Jr. joined the operation and the name was changed to Merritt Wrecking Company. "The honored senior partner is still hale and hearty at age sixty-two," an acquaintance bragged, "while the son was trained to the business from childhood, and combines his energy and ability with the ripe experience of his father to form an organization of commanding influence, eminent popularity, and solid worth."

How much of the *Alice Buck*'s wreck was salvaged is unknown. What is recorded is the memory of the disaster. As with the *Aculeo*, the

The famous Merritt Wrecking Company, established by Capt. Israel J. Merritt in 1860, was dispatched to salvage cargo from the wrecked Alice Buck. American Publishing & Engraving Company.

ship had personal meaning for and captured the imagination of local artist Galen Wolf.

Often passing coastal harbors, the *Alice Buck* was a familiar sight. Wolf grew up remembering the story of the vessel's unhappy end as his grandfather had told it. He recalled a tale of a disastrous voyage, of a ship overtaken by ferocious waves, and of a crew lost in despair.

His painting, "The Wreck," depicts a young boy's woeful discovery at the water's edge. "It was forlorn," Wolf wrote, "and had the desperate appeal of the doomed and deserted."

The once proud ship was now a broken, seaweed-covered hulk. The *Alice Buck* lay forgotten, remembered only by shrieking seabirds.

As with the Aculeo, *the* Alice Buck *stirred the imagination of local artist Galen Wolf. His rendering, "The Wreck," captures the ship's disastrous end.* Allen Bunes & Shannon Nottestad.

7

FORTUNE
AND
MISFORTUNE

NOVEMBER 4, 1890

The lumber schooner *Argonaut* played an important role in developing commerce on the Pacific Coast. Although the vessel wrecked along Montara's rugged shoreline, the experience was not completely unpleasant for her hardy crew.

Sawmills and Sails

During the half century between the Civil War and World War I, the Pacific Coast lumber trade emerged as one of the world's great maritime industries. As settlements spread rapidly throughout the West, the demand for construction materials spiked accordingly. To accommodate this need, hundreds of tiny hamlets with bustling sawmills popped up along the coasts of California, Oregon, and Washington.

Originally, lumber was shipped in old square-riggers, but these large, aging ships proved inefficient for hauling lumber along Pacific shores. They required a large crew and were difficult to maneuver in small ports. Wooden steam schooners soon replaced sailing ships for the hard and treacherous work of loading lumber among the coast's rocks and cliffs. "You couldn't use a deepwater skipper for that kind of work," a former schooner master disclosed. "He would die of fright. Sailing right up to the cliffs, you've got to get used to it. A deepwater man never did."

Schooners were among the first vessels developed in America. With their speed, graceful lines, and relative ease of handling, they became popular as cargo ships. Although the term schooner, meaning "to skim along the surface," was not commonly used until the eighteenth century, this type of vessel evolved in Dutch waters in the seventeenth century. The story is that at the launch of such a boat in 1714, an admirer exclaimed, "the hull scooned upon the water." The proud owner agreed, "Then a sc(h)ooner she shall be!"

A sturdy breed of ship, lumber schooners featured huge unobstructed holds. They were also crafted with the stability to carry more than half their cargo on deck. Lumber was usually loaded not only in the hold, but to a considerable height on deck as well. The crew worked the vessel from atop the towering pile.

Between 1870 and 1905, ever larger schooners transported billions of board feet of lumber for the West Coast's successive construction booms. Before the era ended, the shipyards of California's San Francisco and Humboldt bays, Oregon's Coos Bay, and Washington's Gray's Harbor had launched over 300 three- and four-masted schooners and upwards of 500 two-masted schooners. "They were an ingenious adaptation to the steep coastline of America's northwest," one observer noted, "and could anchor just offshore."

One of these schooners was the *Argonaut*. Built in 1880 at San Francisco by A.M. Simpson & Company, the vessel measured 185 tons, and was 105 feet long with a thirty foot beam and depth of nine feet. The little ship served her master well, helping to build cities as well as a financial empire for her owner, Asa Mead Simpson.

On A Quest

Born in Brunswick, Maine in 1826, Simpson spent his youth on his father's farm with five younger brothers and sisters. At seventeen, he was apprenticed to a shipbuilder, becoming a master in the trade four years later. Using his meager savings, Simpson bought a small interest in the trading vessel *Birmingham*. When gold fever struck California in 1849, he boarded the ship with two brothers, Louis and Isaiah. Like so many other eager young "Argonauts" or adventurers who engage on a quest, the trio rounded Cape Horn in search of their fortune.

Wooden steam schooners, like the Argonaut *and a sister ship pictured here, replaced sailing schooners for the hard and dangerous work of loading lumber along the California coast.* Oregon Historical Society.

A few weeks of mining in California's rugged Sierra Nevada Mountains convinced Simpson that his fortune lay elsewhere. Initially, his prospects seemed dim. Although his diggings netted him fifty ounces of gold dust or about $1,500, half was lost quickly in a loan to a firm that went bankrupt and the other half was stolen by a thief. He lost his interest in the *Birmingham*, too, when she was dispatched back to Maine and wrecked off the coast of Chile. Simpson would later say of these and other setbacks, "My life's work has been getting knocked down and getting on my feet again."

Undaunted, he built his first lumberyard in Stockton, California, peddling the unsold lumber that had been part of the *Birmingham*'s cargo. His real fortune, he decided, was to be made selling lumber, food, and other supplies to mining camps. After enticing his brothers to join him, he formed A.M Simpson & Company, also known as Simpson Brothers.

Seeing further opportunities in the Pacific Northwest, Simpson built a sawmill in Astoria, Oregon in 1851. Over the next two years, ten to fifteen thousand board feet of lumber were turned out daily for use as plank sidewalks in San Francisco. He also salvaged the *Potomac*, a vessel in which he owned a small interest and which wrecked at Astoria. His brother, Louis, refitted and loaded the ship with the mill's lumber and pilings for the San Francisco market.

In 1856, plans were underway to expand the company's operations to Coos Bay, the largest natural harbor on Oregon's coast. Louis sailed with the schooner *Quadratus* to take machinery to start Simpson's sawmill there. While attempting to cross the wide, shallow bar at the mouth of the harbor, the schooner grounded. Knowing that the battering swells would soon destroy the vessel, Louis attempted to row a young woman passenger and her child ashore, but their lifeboat capsized in the breakers and all three drowned.

"Weeks after the accident, long after it became apparent that the ocean would not yield up his brother's body," one biographer revealed, "Asa continued to comb the beach each day, walking along the sand in the coat, tie, and stovepipe hat that he always wore."

Ironically, others aboard the *Quadratus* were saved and much of the mill equipment was salvaged. The Simpson mill began operation late in 1856. A few months later while still absorbing the loss of Louis, Simpson suffered another trauma. His brother, Isaiah, was killed when the lumber schooner *Michigone* foundered at Cape Disappointment off the Oregon coast.

Asa Mead Simpson, who built the Argonaut *for his business in 1880, was known as the "Lumber King of the Pacific."* Oregon Historical Society.

This sawmill and shipyard in Oregon was only one of A.M. Simpson & Company's many timber mills, shipyards, and retail outlets along the Pacific Coast. Oregon Historical Society.

Because of his personal calamities, Simpson established the first lifesaving station built in Southern Oregon on Cape Arago Island. Located at the entrance to Coos Bay Harbor, this one-man station saved thirty-five souls over a ten-year period.

Lumber King of the Pacific

Simpson persevered, and by 1860 had laid the foundation of a vast commercial realm. Company holdings not only included lumberyards in Stockton, Sacramento, and San Francisco, a large floating dock on San Francisco Bay, and the first shipyard at Coos Bay, but also the first sawmill and shipyard at Gray's Harbor, the only deepwater port on the Washington coast.

"Asa was astute in his holdings. He had timber mills, shipyards, and retail outlets up and down the Pacific Coast. He never carried insurance and covered his own losses," his grandson, Michael Simpson, commented. "He was also a frugal man who didn't waste materials. Once, a hitching rail fell apart at one of the Sacramento outlets and the yard foreman rebuilt it with new rather than old lumber. When he heard Asa was coming, he mixed some mud on the rail so Asa wouldn't know it was new."

At one time, Simpson was manufacturing more lumber than anyone else on the West Coast. "He's the big boss in San Francisco," a colleague declared. "He's the Lumber King of the Pacific Coast." While most industry tycoons would be content with this title, Capt. Simpson, as he was now known, was not. He saw opportunities to create overseas markets in Africa, China, Japan, and Russia. For this, he needed more than his fleet of schooners. He needed ocean-going ships. From 1859 to 1903, he built fifty-six world-class tall ships, including the only true clipper ship built on the West Coast, the *Western Shore*.

In 1906, San Francisco's devastating earthquake and resulting fire took its toll on Simpson and his ventures. Although his fine house on Pacific Avenue was spared, his furniture factory, lumberyard, and office building were destroyed, causing a loss of $350,000. Characteristically, Simpson took the setback philosophically. "If catastrophe overtakes me at a certain point," he shrugged, "work goes on at other points."

Nine years later, Simpson died at the age of eighty-nine. With an estate valued at over $20,000,000, he was one of the wealthiest men in California. His far-flung enterprises included interests in woolen mills, real estate, and banking. He owned a fleet of more than sixty sailing vessels and tugs, and over forty thousand acres of virgin timberland in Oregon and Washington. Unfortunately, he was remembered as a man who was "wiry, crusty, and determined to succeed. He was a domineering tycoon who sometimes bullied partners, managers, and captains."

Continual Fog

Over the sixty-five years that Simpson built and managed his lumber and shipping empire, he was haunted by disaster. Two brothers were killed. Several lumber operations were leveled by fire. He also lost thirty-four ships, including the *Argonaut* which ran into a reef at Point Montara on November 4, 1890. The schooner was seven days out of Coos Bay carrying 200,000 feet of lumber and five ninety-foot ships' spars.

"We had fog continually during the voyage and were unable to take an observation," Capt. George C. Lovdal later related. "While steering a course for San Francisco, I struck a strong southerly current which took the vessel eighteen miles out of her course. Hearing the Point Montara fog signal, I took it to be Point Bonita and accordingly laid my course east by southeast to enter the heads."

Perched on a 300 foot cliff on the north side of the Golden Gate, Point Bonita Lighthouse was established in 1855. The first fog signal on the West Coast was placed there, too. Originally, it was an ear-shattering twenty-four pound cannon fired every half-hour when the fog rolled in. The following year, it was replaced by an automated bell. Since the sound of Point Bonita's fog bell would have been quite different than that of Point Montara's steam-whistle, it's difficult to understand Capt. Lovdal's confusion.

At 7:00 A.M., breakers appeared unexpectedly. Before the ship could be brought about, she struck heavily on a reef, disabling her rudder. Although the shore lay just a few yards away, nothing was visible. Capt. Lovdal fired a pistol and blew the ship's horn until the fog lifted.

Keeper David R. Splaine from the Point Montara fog station ran down to the beach to render aid. A Civil War veteran, Splaine served for some years as an assistant keeper at several West Coast lighthouses, including Point Montara. In 1894, he would become the first keeper at the new Ballast Point Lighthouse at the entrance to San Diego Harbor.

With the help of Jurgen Wienke, a local hotel proprietor, Splaine launched a small boat. Rowing through the heavy surf, the duo arrived

Keeper David R. Splaine of the Point Montara fog signal station ran to the rescue when the Argonaut *wrecked nearby.* Grace Killean Collection, Cabrillo National Monument.

near enough to the *Argonaut* to communicate with the stranded vessel's skipper. Capt. Lovdal admitted, "That's when we found our locality."

A few of the crew left the schooner in Splaine's little boat. After establishing a line ashore, they used a pulley to bring the rest of crew and their belongings safely to land.

A local newspaper described the scene, "The crew, consisting of two mates and five seamen, were on the bluff above the beach drying their clothing and putting their baggage in ship shape."

Down on the beach were a number of spectators. "The scene at the wreck had a gala appearance," one account said. "Hundreds of people were on the shore during the day. The beach might have resembled that of Cape May in its most fashionable season, so numerous and varied were the crowds on the sands and the rocks."

Last Delivery

As it happened, a local election was in progress. The people of Montara were attired in their finest wear and a festive mood blanketed the town. In keeping with the cordial atmosphere, the wife of Dr. G.S. Smith invited the bedraggled crew to her house and prepared a substantial dinner. The seamen plunged eagerly into the celebratory whirl as though nothing had happened.

A reporter who had rushed to the shipwreck scene from out of town found the captain feasting on chicken at the Methodist ladies' election supper. The reporter wrote, "The captain remarked that he had been shipwrecked six times, but never before had he been cast up among so many kind people, such pretty women, and so much good grub."

Half a mile south, the abandoned *Argonaut* lay wedged between the rocks, all but forgotten. Keeper Splaine sent his son to town with dispatches for the Merchant's Exchange. The following day, a tug arrived and made several attempts to free the battered schooner. Efforts proved futile and the vessel, valued at $4,000, was given up as lost.

"This is the third wreck at this particular place, which seems to be the most dangerous on this part of the coast," newspapers commented. "Owing to the short distance between the fog whistles on Point Bonita and Point Montara, they can easily be mistaken one for the other, which accounts for the present disaster."

On November 8, what was left of the *Argonaut* and its cargo was sold at auction at the Merchant's Exchange in San Francisco. Purchased by the wrecking firm of Rogers & Company, a crew was put to work taking off the sails and rigging, preparatory to removing the cargo. The lumber in the hold was almost a total loss. The deck load, consisting of 100,000 feet of lumber and the five ships' spars, was saved. The stalwart schooner had completed her last delivery.

Days later, debris from the wreck littered the beach. Pieces of the ship, split boards, and rasped timbers all attested to the awful power of the waves. Shattered upon the jagged rocks, the *Argonaut* splintered into pieces and floated away.

8

RED RECORD SHIP

MARCH 13, 1898

T he *T.F. Oakes* was one of the most notorious ships to ever sail. Her reputation failed to improve, even after she was renamed the *New York*.

Nothing is Right

Only three large full-rigged iron-hulled sailing ships were built in the United States: the *Tillie E. Starbuck*, the *T.F. Oakes*, and the *Clarence S. Bement*. Unfortunately, the careers of each of these vessels was so discouraging that it marked the end of American efforts to construct iron sailing vessels almost before it began. The *T.F. Oakes* received the greatest notoriety, for her odyssey was anything but tranquil.

Named after Thomas Fletcher Oakes, president of Northern Pacific Railway, the *T.F. Oakes* was constructed in 1883 for William H. Starbuck, a prominent New York shipping merchant. Originally, she was designed to transport materials for constructing railroads in the Pacific Northwest. When the Northern Pacific Railway was completed in the winter of 1883, Starbuck moved the vessel into other trade.

Starbuck was impressed by the theoretical superiority of iron over wood as a shipbuilding material and dreamed of revolutionizing

American shipping. Using iron, he explained, had "the benefit of increased carrying capacity, better insurance, and stronger ships."

Built by the newly formed American Shipbuilding Company of Philadelphia, the *T.F. Oakes* was 255 feet long, nearly 41 feet wide, and measured 1,997 tons. Valued at $135,000, the vessel was painted black and white, had a round stern, two decks, three masts, and an eagle on the bow. Veteran seaman Peter Johnson called her, "The finest looking sailing ship I had ever seen."

The *T. F. Oakes* was delivered rapidly, entering the water just 150 days after the keel was laid. At her launching, Henry H. Gorringe, a former naval commander and head of American Shipbuilding, boasted, "I have leased this shipyard for the purpose of building the merchant marine of the future. Our successful launch today is only a beginning. No yard in this country has finer facilities for doing work expeditiously and well than we do here."

Sadly, the iron ship would never live up to everyone's high praise. She proved a heavy, dull, and slow sailer as well as an unlucky vessel. She was top heavy, carrying 11,000 square yards of canvas, and when she passed under New York's Brooklyn Bridge, all three of her masts had to be lowered.

With Capt. John B. Clift at the helm, her first voyage broke all records for the longest passage, a leisurely 195 days, from New York to San Francisco. Bound for China on her second voyage, the *T.F. Oakes* was caught in a typhoon, thrown on her beam ends, and nearly wrecked. A passing steamer rescued the crippled ship and towed her into Hong Kong.

"The trouble started in the model before the keel was laid; it continued in the building, in the placing of the masts and the proportioning of spars and cutting of canvas," one observer declared. "Nothing is right and in balance, and no matter how you drive or jockey in handling a ship, you can never get out of her what is not in her."

Shipboard Injustices

For the next decade, the *T. F. Oakes* plodded the seas earning the reputation of a ship on which "blows were plenty and food was scarce." When a new skipper, Capt. Edward W. Reed took command, her record failed to improve. Capt. Reed had a stormy career aboard the vessel and was often accused of abusing his crew. Broadly publicized in the "Red

Henry H. Gorringe, a former naval command-
er and head of the newly formed American
Shipbuilding Company of Philadelphia, Penn-
sylvania, built the T.F. Oakes *in 1883.* Author's
collection.

One of only three full-rigged iron-hulled sailing ships ever built in the U.S., the T.F. Oakes *was also one of the most notorious vessels ever to sail.* Maine Maritime Museum.

Record" of the *Coast Seamen's Journal*, the charges did little to enhance the ship's esteem.

The *Coast Seamen's Journal* was first published in 1887 by the Coast Seamen's Union, then two years old and with an active membership of 2,000 men. The Journal had always run stories of shipboard injustices, but a new feature appeared in 1894. A litany of brutality cases were grouped together in a column called the "Red Record." The article was subtitled, "Being a Bare Outline of Some of the Cases of Cruelty Perpetrated Upon American Seamen." It bore as its trademark a red ink engraving of a fist with a bloody belaying pin.

"Something must be done to wipe out this shameful blot upon an honorable profession," Walter J. Macarthur, the *Journal*'s editor, stressed. "In the name of justice and humanity we call upon our readers to do what lies in their power, particularly by making the facts widely known, toward the abolition of the seagoing Legrees!"

After a voyage in 1893, Capt. Reed was charged with cruelty. Six seamen gave evidence in court and displayed wounds they claimed he inflicted. Although many spectators in the court expressed indignation and confidence of a conviction, Capt. Reed made no defense. The jury returned the verdict that, "A shipmaster has the right to beat a seaman who is unruly." The *Coast Seamen's Journal* commented that the case demonstrated "the dangerous powers vested in ships' officers."

Following another crossing in 1895, Capt. Reed was charged with "extreme brutality and murder." The crew testified that Frederick Owens, an able seaman who complained of sickness, was assaulted, dragged out of the forecastle, and compelled to work during bitterly cold weather off Cape Horn. They contended that Capt. Reed ordered Owens to "walk the deck, even though he couldn't work." Owens was given no medical attention except a dose of salts and a mustard plaster and died two days later. Capt. Reed was acquitted.

Disastrous Passage

A particularly disastrous passage from Hong Kong to New York occurred in 1896. On July 5, the *T.F. Oakes* cleared Hong Kong with a cargo of hides and skins and a complement of twenty-seven, including Capt. Reed and his wife, Hannah. A week out of Hong Kong, the ship was caught in a succession of typhoons which blew her 500 miles off

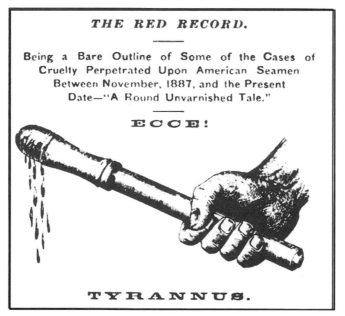

The "Red Record," a list of brutality cases against seamen, first appeared in 1887. It bore as its trademark a red ink engraving of a fist with a bloody belaying pin. Coast Seamen's Journal.

Hannah Reed, wife of Capt. Edward W. Reed, who commanded the T.F. Oakes, *was hailed for her skill in steering the troubled ship during a disastrous voyage in 1896.* Ron Druett.

course to the northeast. As a result, Capt. Reed decided not to take the usual course around the Cape of Good Hope in South Africa, sailing instead, toward Cape Horn in South America. The new route was five to seven thousand miles farther.

"After many never-ending days and nights we found ourselves battling gales. Head gales mostly, with bitter weather, driving rain, icy sleet, and blinding snow. Always soaked to the skin and always hungry. God in Heaven, how hungry we were," seaman Hans Arro recalled. "With huge waves continually flooding over her decks, the ship was wet and cold. And how cold and dank was our leaky fo'c'sle with no stove to warm and dry it."

The voyage took over eight months. During that time, Capt. Reed was partially paralyzed by a stroke and many of the weary crew fell ill with scurvy. The disease progressed rapidly, killing six men, and disabling everyone else but the Second Mate and Mrs. Reed. The tormented ship crawled up the Brazilian coast with Mrs. Reed, "a sturdy, grey haired, slate-eyed woman of fifty," at the helm. Daily rations were cut to six ounces of bread and a gulp of water per person. While off Trinidad, another vessel, the *Governor Robie*, supplied a few provisions but conditions continued to worsen.

"The man Abrams could hardly speak and his legs were so swollen that it was a wonder that he could drag himself about the deck. The Captain and Third Officer Eagan were too helpless to leave their bunks, and Mrs. Reed was almost as bad," one account said. "Forward, eleven men lay starving and helpless in their bunks, most of them toothless owing to the scurvy. They were so weak that they slid from side to side on their straw mattresses on every roll of the ship."

On March 15, 1897 the blue glare of the stricken vessel's distress signal was sighted by the British tanker *Kasbek*. In reply to a hail from the *Kasbek*, a voice from the *T.F. Oakes* shouted back, "Can't heave to – all dead and sick. For heaven's sake stand by and send us a boat."

A handful of the *Kasbek*'s crew remained aboard the *T.F. Oakes*. For three days the iron ship staggered alongside the tanker. When the heavy winds and seas subsided, the *Kasbek* attached a towing hawser to pull the *T.F. Oakes* into port. Finally, on March 21st anchor was dropped near a New York quarantine station. By this time, the *T.F. Oakes* was 249 days out from China and listed as missing. According to one account, "All hope for her reappearance had been abandoned."

For her skill in steering the troubled ship, Lloyd's awarded Mrs. Reed its Silver Medal for Meritorious Service. Capt. Reed, on the other hand, was charged with maliciously withholding food from the crew. During a trial before a New York District Court, members of Capt. Reed's crew gave vivid accounts of deprivation and beatings, and read letters written by sailors who had died during the voyage. Many were unable to walk unassisted to the witness stand. Capt. Reed himself limped into the courtroom. Paralysis still affected his speech, but he denied all allegations.

The case was dismissed on the grounds that due to the extreme length of the passage, shortage of food was unavoidable. However, that did not end the dispute. Eight sailors pressed charges against Capt. Reed for neglecting to supply proper and sufficient food. They were each awarded $362.25.

Capt. Reed retired from sea life. The following winter, his home in Haverhill, Massachusetts burned down. The captain escaped in his nightshirt but caught pneumonia and died in March 1899. The cause of the fire was never known, but it was rumored that some of his crew had a hand in it as retaliation for his treatment of them.

A Miserable Time

While the *T.F. Oakes* was at sea, she was purchased by Lewis Luckenbach. His steamship company was one of the most long-lived and successful shipping enterprises in the United States. After building his fortune by pioneering tug-and-barge transport of coal from Norfolk, Virginia to New England, Luckenbach became a major force in the intercoastal trade between the Atlantic and Pacific shores.

Luckenbach received delivery of the *T.F. Oakes* once she reached port. He was no doubt stunned by the unexpected lengthy voyage and the subsequent courtroom debacle. Realizing that it would be impossible to lure sailors to a vessel with a checkered history, Luckenbach changed the ship's name to the *New York*. He also hired the experienced shipmaster Thomas Peabody, who "was regarded as a high class navigator, a driver, and a strict disciplinarian."

After a thorough overhaul, the ship sailed from New York on May 18, 1897. Bound for Shanghai and then Hong Kong, the trip went without incident. On the return voyage to San Francisco, the vessel carried Capt. Peabody, his wife, Clara, and eight-year-old daughter, Claire, twenty crew, and a rich cargo of coffee, dry goods, firecrackers, flour, garlic,

Capt. Thomas Peabody fought gales and heavy fog until the T.F. Oakes, *newly renamed the* New York, *crashed broadside onto the beach at Half Moon Bay in 1898.* San Francisco Call.

green beans, hemp, peanut oil, pineapples, porcelains, rattan furniture, silk, spices, tapioca rice, tea, tobacco, and wine.

Unhappily, the vessel's new-found good luck was fleeting. Leaving Hong Kong harbor on January 14, 1898, the *New York* was plagued by unceasing storms. "From the first day we had a miserable time. Our ship ran into storm after storm," Claire Peabody wrote later. "The crew, disheartened, whispered among themselves that maybe the *New York* was a jinx-ship. Some of the men even went so far as to predict they would never see San Francisco harbor again."

About nine hundred miles off the California coast, the vessel ran into a furious squall which snapped the main mast. With no extra spars aboard, the crew did their best to patch the damage, but it was not enough. "Her steering had been bad enough before," seaman Paul Scharrenberg stated, "but from that night the good ship could not be made to readily respond to her helm."

Gales continued to batter the ship as she struggled up the California coast. In the early morning hours of March 13, 1898, the *New York* became lost in heavy fog and was driven broadside onto the beach in Half Moon Bay. The misguided vessel missed her destination by a mere thirty miles. "The only explanation I can give of the disaster is the fact of the extremely contrary current along the coast at that time," Capt. Peabody shrugged. "The seaman aloft could see nothing. I thought I was a little farther north, and that Point Bonita Light, for which I was looking, was on my bow."

Over the next few hours, the *New York* settled in the sand about two hundred yards from shore. Capt. Peabody and his crew made preparations to launch the two undamaged lifeboats. Carrying the captain's wife and daughter and eight men, the first boat narrowly escaped destruction against the *New York*'s iron hull, filled with water from the crashing waves, and nearly capsized. Scores of local residents who had dashed to the scene formed a human chain into the sea and snatched the helpless group from the undercurrent.

A second boat with ten crew was successfully launched but not without mishap. Heavy seas hurled the ship's cook between the craft and the davits, fracturing his leg at the knee. Three men, including Capt. Peabody, still remained aboard the *New York*. Several attempts were made to launch a boat back to rescue them, but the turbulent surf prevailed. Only at daybreak did the captain and the last of his crew manage to reach shore.

After she wrecked, the New York *sank twenty feet into the sand before vanishing entirely.* San Mateo County History Museum.

The tug *Reliance*, under the command of Capt. Gilbert Brokaw, was dispatched from San Francisco but heavy surf and strong southwest winds made it impossible to get closer than half a mile from the stranded ship. "The beach at Half Moon Bay," W.C. Callip, the *New York*'s first mate, observed, "will in all probability be her graveyard."

However, the sturdy tug averted another disaster. Bound from San Francisco to Cork, Ireland with a cargo of wheat, the British four-master *Clan Galbraith* came dangerously close to where the *New York* lay. Capt. Brokaw hailed the vessel and kept the *Reliance* by her side until she passed safely. "It was touch and go with her," he acknowledged. "I delayed my departure for San Francisco, thinking every minute she would require my assistance."

An Unpleasant Memory

Meanwhile, the ill-fated *New York* sank deeper and deeper until she lay buried in twenty-three feet of sand. By March 16th, the iron ship was filled with water, the main hatch was broken, cabin windows were smashed, furniture was awash, the forecastle was completely gutted, and the vessel had a decided list. "The tapioca rice in her hold had burst the deck and might force the hull apart," the *New York Maritime Register* reported. "The vessel had fallen over to starboard and the seas were breaking over her. Her back was broken."

The *New York*'s cargo, worth $500,000, was sold at auction for $5,600 on March 24th. Two days later, U.S. Customs officials set up a crude shanty on the beach. The structure was composed primarily of the ship's hatches, which had washed ashore. Tents were also erected, and three cables were rigged between the ship and the shore. "The inspectors at the scene found it necessary to keep a close watch upon the goods saved from the wreck," one newspaper disclosed. "The beach is infested with thieves, who prowl in the night as well as during the day."

Before the Customs inspectors arrived to take possession of the cargo, local residents claimed many souvenirs from the ship. "My father, along with other young men, went out to claim relics," Mrs. Ethel Knapp Neate confessed. "I have in my home the big arm chair taken from the captain's cabin."

Several boxes of hand-painted chinaware also disappeared, finding their way into Half Moon Bay homes. Some still survive in excellent condition today. Horace Nelson took possession of the ship's bell. After tolling out so many hours at sea, it hung on the water tower of his ranch where it was used to call the hands to their meals.

Along with six of his crew, Capt. Peabody made several trips to the doomed vessel to bring ashore personal effects of the sailors and his daughter's pet birds. Peabody and his family took such a liking to the coastside that they settled in nearby Moss Beach for several years.

The following month, the *New York* was stripped of all her fittings and ornamentation. Everything of value was taken, leaving her a skeleton in the sand. Soon, all traces of the infamous ship vanished. Seaman Paul Scharrenberg, who served on the *New York* and later became editor of the *Coast Seamen's Journal*, declared, "The wreckers and breakers made scrap iron out of her and left her a more or less unpleasant memory to deepwater sailors the world over."

It was a shameful epitaph for a scandalous ship.

The wreck of the New York *was celebrated in 1948 at a Fifty Year Reunion of survivors and family members. Paul Scharrenberg, a former seaman aboard the vessel, is at the rear of the group between two other men.* Carl W. May.

9

AN OUTRAGE

SEPTEMBER 23, 1899

The *Leelanaw* was one of the most famous cargo ships in America. She suffered only a scratch when she bumped into the reef at Point Montara. Her fatal wound would come a short time later, during the first stirrings of World War I. Part of her legacy would be a lighthouse.

Early Trade

The earliest cargo ships date back to the ancient world when the Phoenicians carried trade goods by vessel across the Mediterranean and into the Atlantic Ocean. Later, the Chinese used flat boats called junks to ferry merchandise to Indonesia and India. During the Middle Ages, the Venetians owned a huge merchant fleet that transported commodities through Europe's natural waterways.

In the 1600s, the Dutch operated a globe-circling shipping service for merchants of Western Europe. Throughout the 1700s and 1800s, many a captain set out to sea to explore uncharted territory in search of foodstuffs, gold, perfume, silk, spice, and other items for trade. American packets and clipper ships carried cargos of farm, forest, and fish products from coast to coast and continent to continent.

The steamer Earnwell, *later the* Leelanaw, *was built in 1886 as the pioneer vessel of the Earn-Line Steamship Company.* Philadelphia Maritime Exchange.

After 1850, the development of an efficient steam engine allowed world trade to increase tenfold over the next sixty years. The cargo steamship of the late nineteenth century varied in size and shape, from huge liners running between Europe and the Far East to the tiny coasters that supplied growing communities with local necessities.

As America grew in economic and industrial strength, ships of ever-increasing size were needed to transport goods to its burgeoning cities, as well as to ports overseas. Vessels like the *Leelanaw* were designed specifically to haul bulk loads of materials ranging from coal, cotton, grain, iron, lumber, and sugar to military supplies and horses.

Cargo ships may not seem a very romantic topic, but these hard working vessels are an important segment of American maritime history. Even today, ninety percent of the world's commerce moves by water. Thousands of cargo ships still ply the seas each year carrying millions of tons of goods and materials to ports far and wide.

Pioneer Cargo Ship

Under the name *Earnwell*, the *Leelanaw* was built in 1886 at Newcastle, England by Palmer's Shipbuilding and Iron Company. The vessel measured 1,496 tons, was 280 feet long, 36 feet wide, 23 feet deep, and had the capacity of carrying 2,500 tons of freight.

The steamer was the pioneer vessel of the Earn-Line Steamship Company. Established by Alfred Earnshaw in 1885, the firm transported iron ore to North Atlantic ports from Cuba. There, in cooperation with the Pennsylvania Steel Company and the Bethlehem Iron Company, Earnshaw had developed the first successful iron ore mine.

Over the next decade, the company expanded its interests, carrying cargos of coal to ports around the Caribbean. In 1896, while en route to Philadelphia, the *Earnwell* was driven ashore near Panama in a heavy storm. After considerable effort, she was floated by a wrecking steamer and towed to Newport News, Virginia where she was declared a total loss. Israel J. Merritt, Sr., who had salvaged a portion of the doomed *Alice Buck*, bought the vessel and sold it to the Saginaw Steamship Company. The steamer was towed to New York and then to New Jersey for repairs and renamed the *Leelanaw*.

The Saginaw Steamship Company was organized in 1890 by Arthur Hill, a prominent lumber merchant of Saginaw, Michigan. Joining him in the venture were Frank W. Wheeler, the proprietor of F.W. Wheeler

& Company, an important Great Lakes firm engaged in wood and steel shipbuilding; Samuel Holmes, a marine engineer and the leading shipbroker of New York City; and James Jerome, also of Saginaw.

The company operated a total of five vessels, including the *Leelanaw*, all named for cities and counties in Michigan. Each of the freighters was designed to carry coal, cotton, iron, lumber, sugar, and other commodities. Originally, the firm announced its intention to build ships for use in the coal-carrying trade out of Baltimore. However, after the first ships were launched, the enterprise responded to the high demand and high profit potential of freighting on the Pacific Coast.

True to her purpose, the *Leelanaw* served in assorted capacities. During 1898, the vessel made two trips to Alaska in the gold rush service, later transferring to the coal run between San Francisco and Seattle. In 1899, she began regular transpacific voyages to Manila via Honolulu, carrying horses and supplies to U.S. forces stationed there after the Spanish-American War. One of these voyages went terribly amiss.

Rolling and Bumping

Under the command of Capt. A. J. Storrs, the *Leelanaw* left San Francisco for Manila on September 2, 1899 carrying a cargo of military supplies, primarily canned goods, and 200 cavalry horses. "After leaving the port, distemper developed among the horses," reports said later, "and so many of the animals died, that the ship put into Honolulu and landed the commissary stores and the surviving horses."

Leaving the sick and panic-stricken animals to recuperate in an Army corral, the *Leelanaw* sailed back to San Francisco for additional mounts. Nearing the California coast, she encountered heavy haze. "For three days, so thick and constant was the fog that no observations could be taken," a local newspaper reported. As a result, Capt. Storrs was further to the southeast than his calculations indicated.

On September 23rd, Capt. Storrs believed the ship to be near the Farallon Islands. Just before 5:00 P.M., he heard the blast of a foghorn and rang the engine room to reduce speed to dead slow so that he could identify the sound. Too late, Capt. Storrs realized that the foghorn's signal was more irregular than that of the Farallones.

The *Leelanaw* struck the reefs just south of Point Montara and stranded head-on, held fast beneath the bow. A quick examination showed water seeping in through a break in one of the forward ballast

After being driven ashore in a storm in 1896, the Earn-well *was re-floated, repaired, and renamed the* Leela-naw. *In 1899, the steamer struck the reefs just south of Point Montara.* Author's collection.

The sinking by Germany of neutral ships like the Leelanaw *and the* William P. Frye, *depicted here, was a major factor in America's decision to enter World War I.* State Library of Victoria.

tanks. Capt. Storrs wasted no time setting the crew to work at the pumps. Luckily, they encountered little trouble keeping the tank relatively clear of water. Around 11:30 P.M., the captain rang full speed astern in an attempt to back off the reef. Rolling and bumping, the bruised steamer floated free and limped up the coast to San Francisco.

Hobbling into the bay the following morning, the tug *Alert* hovered nearby ready for any emergency. The steamer's government charter was cancelled and repairs were scheduled at the owner's expense. Damaged more seriously than first anticipated, the *Leelanaw* was placed in drydock where she remained for twenty-three days. "It was found that the ragged rock had torn a hole in her bottom," one account noted. "In addition to the leak, the vessel was badly strained by her experience on the reef." Nearly thirty hull plates were repaired or replaced. At the end of October, she was re-chartered to transport additional horses to Manila.

Torpedoed Into History

The *Leelanaw* continued in this service until 1901, after which she returned to the San Francisco to Seattle coal trade route and began runs between San Francisco and Panama. In 1902, the Saginaw Steamship Company changed its name to the Michigan Steamship Company which dissolved in 1908. Before closing its doors, the firm sold the *Leelanaw* to the Pacific Freight Company of Tacoma, Washington, which in turn sold the vessel to the Leelanaw Steamship Company in 1911.

Four years later, she was purchased by the Harris-Irby Cotton Company and operated by the Harby Steamship Company. In May of 1915, the *Leelanaw* sailed from New York under the command of Capt. Eugene B. Delk with a load of cotton intended for Gothenburg, Sweden. From there, the cargo would be shipped by rail to Moscow, Russia. According to later reports, an uneasy Capt. Delk "made a last minute decision before sailing for Europe and prevented his wife, who normally accompanied her husband at sea, from being on the steamship."

The captain had made a wise decision. In 1915, England, France, and Russia, were at war with Germany while the U.S. remained neutral. As a result, British authorities often intercepted vessels in the Atlantic in order to lessen the possibility of merchandise falling into German hands. Thus, the *Leelanaw* was intercepted and diverted to the port of Kirkwall, Scotland, the capital of the Orkney Islands. She was released on the understanding that she would proceed directly to Archangel, Russia.

On June 26th, the cotton was discharged at Archangel and a cargo consisting of 1,000 tons of flax was loaded for Belfast, Ireland. Having been converted to an oil-burning steamship, the *Leelanaw* was unable to obtain enough oil at Archangel to take her back to New York. Capt Delk accepted the cargo for Belfast where the ship's bunker tanks could be refilled for the trip across the Atlantic.

The *Leelanaw* set sail for Belfast on July 17th, with a complement of thirty-three officers and crew, mostly American. Eight days later, the captain noticed a German submarine.

"We were sixty miles northwest of Kirkwall when I observed two steamers to the north and heard a shot fired," Capt. Delk recalled. "Soon, I saw a submarine (*U-41*) heading toward one of the vessels. Immediately afterward, one of them sank. The submarine fired another shot and started in pursuit of the *Leelanaw*."

Capt. Delk altered his course and decided to run for it, but the submarine made quick headway and fired a shot which fell only 300 yards short of the ship. "I put the helm over and headed toward the submarine, which signaled to us to send our papers aboard," the captain continued. "This I did. The officers and crew were then told to abandon the ship."

When the submarine commander discovered that the *Leelanaw*'s cargo was flax, the crew was instructed to gather their belongings into the ship's lifeboats. Not only was flax on Germany's list of contraband, but this particular cargo was owned by Russia, one of Germany's enemies.

"We got into the boats and rowed away, after which the submarine fired five shots at the starboard side. None of them took effect, as they struck above the water line," Capt. Delk explained. "The submarine then fired a torpedo which hit the steamer amidships and she began to sink at once. As the *Leelanaw* was still above water, more shots were fired into the port side. The second set the steamer afire."

The German commander stood by until the $225,000 vessel vanished beneath the sea. Capt. Delk and his crew were taken aboard the submarine with their boats in tow and delivered to a point eight miles from the coast of Orkney. There, they were ordered back into their boats. As the men began rowing to shore, the submarine slowly disappeared.

Just months apart, the *William P. Frye* and the *Leelanaw* were the first American vessels attacked and sunk by German war craft during World War I. "It's a damnable outrage. I think this is a perfectly hellish condition to which our peace-at-any-price policy has brought us," former President Theodore Roosevelt huffed. "Any man with an ounce of red blood in his body will feel this, a deliberate insult that Germany puts upon us, an insult the more aggravated by reason of the utter senselessness of this latest attack upon an unarmed merchant ship."

The sinking of neutral ships such as the *William P. Frye*, the *Leelanaw*, and the British passenger liner *Lusitania* turned public opinion against Germany and was a major factor in America's eventual decision to join the war in 1917. This would not be the *Leelanaw*'s only legacy.

Final Legacy

A year after the wreck of the *Leelanaw*, a light was established at Point Montara. Sitting only seventy feet above the sea, the lamp was lit on November 26, 1900 and could be seen twelve miles at sea. Curiously, it was merely a red kerosene-fueled lantern, about one foot in diameter and two feet high, hung on a post three hundred feet from the fog signal building. "The light will be red," the Lighthouse Board said, "so as not to be confused with the white light at Point Bonita."

The principal keeper was Nils Henry Hall whose daughter, Mary Elizabeth, was born at the station. She recalled that staples such as flour, rice, and sugar arrived by tender in large cloth sacks. When the sacks were empty, her mother washed them and used the material to make clothes for the Hall's five children. Mary Elizabeth's son, Ed Wardell, grinned, "For years, my mother thought that C&H Sugar made little girl's underclothes."

In 1902, the fog signal building, "being old and dilapidated, was pulled down and rebuilt." A barn and stable, which had been added to the site in 1884, remained, but a new coal house was also built. A lighthouse tower, of sorts, was constructed in 1914. It consisted of a small, fourth order Fresnel lens installed in a simple wooden pyramid tower.

Developed by French physicist Augustin Fresnel (pronounced fra-nel), a revolutionary "beehive" design used glass prisms surrounding a single light source. When the lighthouse was lit, the prisms bent or "refracted" the light through magnifying circles called "bulls-eyes" in the center of each of the larger panels. The resulting beam was five times more powerful than earlier reflector systems.

In 1919, the U.S. Lighthouse Board approved nearly $12,000 to upgrade Point Montara's light to electric and to install a more efficient fog signal apparatus. The U.S. Lighthouse Board reported, "It became necessary owing to its importance as a coast light." By 1928, Point Montara's original pyramid tower had nearly disintegrated and the

A year after the Leelanaw *went aground, the first light was established at Point Montara. In 1914, the wooden pyramid tower shown at the left was installed.* Christopher Bauman.

Point Montara's cast-iron tower, erected in 1928, was transported from Mayo's Beach Lighthouse at Cape Cod, Massachusetts. Christopher Bauman.

current white, conical tower was erected. Just thirty feet high, a recent discovery brought the little sentinel into national prominence.

To understand Point Montara's history, it is also necessary to understand the history of Mayo's Beach Light of Wellfleet, Massachusetts. Overlooking Cape Cod, the first lighthouse at Mayo's Beach was constructed in 1838. It consisted of a short wooden tower and octagonal lantern placed on the roof of a saltbox-style brick building. The dwelling contained three rooms on the first floor and two rooms on the second floor. Set twenty-one feet above the water, ten oil lamps with thirteen-inch parabolic reflectors produced a fixed white light which could be seen twelve miles out at sea. In 1857, the light was refitted with a fourth-order Fresnel lens.

In 1881, a cast-iron tower and a separate keeper's house were built. Even a stronger tower and light couldn't prevent shipwrecks. Over the years, the area's horrendous winter gales claimed hundreds of vessels including the 270-ton brig *Diligence*, the brig *Mary Johnson*, the schooner *Amethyst*, and the schooner turned coal barge *Logan*, whose remains washed up on the beach in 2008.

The tower remained in service until its light was discontinued on March 10, 1922. The station property was sold at auction August 1, 1923 to Capt. Harry Capron. For decades, New England archivists thought the lighthouse had been removed and destroyed. In 2008, intrepid researcher Colleen MacNeney uncovered photos and correspondence that proved the lighthouse had been moved by the Coast Guard from Wellfleet to Yerba Buena, California and eventually to Point Montara. MacNeney exclaimed, "Oh, my gosh! I knew we had found a fact that had been lost to historians."

Built in a foundry in Chelsea, Massachusetts just north of Boston, no one knows how the cast-iron tower was moved. Some speculate that it could have been disassembled bolt by bolt and the pieces transported by rail. Others say it might have been moved mostly intact by ship. In any case, Point Montara is America's only lighthouse to have cast its rays across both Atlantic and Pacific shores.

Point Montara Lighthouse as it stands today. It is America's only lighthouse to have witnessed shipwrecks on both Atlantic and Pacific shores. Julie Barrow.

10

CLYDEBUILT

MARCH 19, 1900

S ometimes, even the best built ship grows tired and troubled. The venerable *City of Florence* wrecked just two hundred yards north of where the infamous *New York* met her demise.

Great Shipbuilding City

Originally a small salmon-fishing village at a crossing point on the sparkling River Clyde, Glasgow, Scotland grew into one of the greatest shipbuilding cities on earth. From the early 1800s into the 1900s, the banks of the Clyde sprouted with shipyards where tens of thousands of men built magnificent ships.

Stretching more than a hundred miles, the Clyde was naturally a shallow waterway, often only two feet deep at low tide. In 1768, a sequence of dikes was built, narrowing the channel and greatly increasing the flow of water, which in turn scoured the bed and deepened the river. In 1812, the Clyde's entry into the world of shipbuilding began when the twenty-eight ton paddle steamer *Comet*, Europe's first sea-going steam ship, was launched at Port Glasgow.

An ad in local newspapers invited passengers to board the new vessel. It claimed, "The subscriber, having at much expense, fitted up a handsome vessel to ply upon the River Clyde from Glasgow, to sail

In the 1860s, the River Clyde in Glasgow, Scotland, was one of the world's pre-eminent shipbuilding centers. "Clydebuilt" vessels such as the City of Florence *were known for their excellence, durability, and reliability.* Author's collection.

by the power of air, wind, and steam, intends that the vessel shall leave Broomielaw on Tuesdays, Thursdays, and Saturdays about mid-day, or such hour thereafter as may answer from the state of the tide, and to leave Greenock on Mondays, Wednesdays, and Fridays in the morning to suit the tide." The fare was "four shillings for the best cabin and three shillings for the second."

The *Comet* made a delivery voyage from Port Glasgow twenty-one miles upriver to Broomielaw, then sailed the twenty-four miles down to Greenock, making five-miles-an-hour against a head-wind. The success of this service quickly inspired competition, and due to its location in the west of the country, Glasgow was well-positioned to send cargo to the West Indies and the United States.

Accordingly, shipyards were established on the Clyde at an extraordinary rate. Soon, the river gained a reputation for producing the best vessels in Britain and emerged as the world's pre-eminent shipbuilding center. "Clydebuilt" became a byword for excellence, durability, and reliability.

Superior Ships

One of the premiere shipbuilders of the day was Charles Connell. After serving an apprenticeship with Robert Steele & Company, he managed the shipyard of Alexander Stephen & Sons. Both were well-established and respected firms on the Clyde. In 1861, Connell formed his own firm initially concentrating on sailing ships.

The enterprise, known as C. Connell & Company, was successful beyond Connell's wildest dreams, delivering vessels such as the *City of Florence* and other passenger and cargo ships to customers around the world. His famous ships include the *Balclutha*, now on display at the San Francisco Maritime Museum. "Well known for high quality," his vessels sailed in the fleets of countless international shipping lines.

The shipyard passed from the Connell family's ownership in 1968 to become part of the Upper Clyde Shipbuilders, finally closing in 1980 after 119 years of shipbuilding. Over 500 ships were launched under the Connell name.

Although the *City of Florence* was built by Charles Connell, she was owned by George Smith, another Scotsman. In partnership with his brother, Robert, Smith established the City Line of Calcutta in 1840 to support their cotton manufacturing firm's expanding trade with India. After purchasing several ready-made ships, they resolved that any further additions to their fleet should be vessels built to their own specifications.

George Smith, who owned the City of Florence, *established a fleet of ships named for cities around the world. The popular company soon became known as "The City Line."* James MacLehose.

"This resolution was steadily adhered to, with the result that a superior type of ship was built," reports said, "and the vessels of the firm rapidly acquired fame for their speed, safety, and regularity."

In 1847 construction of their first vessel was contracted with Tod & Macgregor of Glasgow. When she was launched the following year, the brothers wished to acknowledge the port and dubbed her the *City of Glasgow*. The succeeding ships of their fleet were named after other cities and the company came to be known as "The City Line."

Within a decade, voyages to Chile and the West Indies, Australia, and New Zealand were common. In 1871, the company added steamers to their burgeoning fleet. "For economy of working, carrying power, and speed suited to the trade in which they are employed, the steamers are regarded as holding a foremost place amongst steamship lines," an admirer bragged. "Their safety is proverbial and the well-known preference they command in both goods and passengers is deserved."

George Smith died in 1876, three years after his brother passed away, leaving the business to his son, George, Jr. He was remembered as a man who was "of sharp, quick, and powerful intellect with immense capacity for work."

Unlucky Voyage

The *City of Florence*, a three-masted sailing ship, slid down the ways of the River Clyde in 1867. She had a length of 227 feet, a beam of 34 feet, a depth of 22 feet, and measured 1,246 tons. Although she had several masters, Capt. William "Jock" Leask, who commanded her from 1884 to 1899, was at the helm for almost half her life.

Born in the Orkney Islands off the northern tip of Scotland in 1851, William Leask served the usual seaman's apprenticeship before taking command of his first ship. Described by one biographer as:

> … a man of medium height though broad to the point of ungain-liness, it needed only a glance at the keen gray eyes peering from beneath bushy eyebrows, the determined set of a square lower jaw, to note a man accustomed to command. A quick, alert turn of the head, the lift of shoulders as he walked, arms swinging in seaman-like balance, and the trick of pausing to glance at the weather sky, marked the sailing shipmaster, the man to whom thought and action must be one.

An experienced skipper, Capt. Leask rounded treacherous Cape Horn forty-two times. One of his worst trips aboard the *City of Florence*

Capt. William Leask commanded the City of Florence *for nearly half of her life.* Pat Long.

occurred on a voyage from Antwerp, Belgium carrying 9,590 barrels of cement consigned to Mever, Wilson, & Company. The vessel encountered twenty-eight days of successive gales and hurricanes. Capt. Leask stated simply, "It was an unlucky voyage throughout."

The ship's main mast splintered. Sail after sail flew away in shreds. Mountainous waves pounded the beleaguered vessel, smashing the lifeboats and damaging cabin doors. Deck fastenings were ripped from their ring bolts. The ship's carpenters, Robert Gillies and George Berston, fought valiantly to cope with the damage but continuing storms allowed only slapdash repairs.

Not a man escaped injury. Six of the crew suffered broken arms and cracked ribs. Others had bruises, cuts, and sprains. All were drenched to the bone. Miraculously, no one was washed overboard. Unable to cook anything for days at a time, starvation threatened the bedraggled crew.

Over 180 days after leaving Antwerp, a battered *City of Florence* dragged into San Francisco Bay. "Something closely akin to a wreck was towed through the Golden Gate after dark. She had what looked like board fences in half a dozen places. Much of her rigging was worn and spliced," a local newspaper reported. "Even in the inky darkness that prevailed, the few people who boarded her could read the story of havoc by gale and sea."

On another voyage, the *City of Florence* was sailing in thick fog, sounding her foghorn. The crew thought they heard another foghorn, dead ahead. Through the mist, it appeared as if a ship was on the horizon, showing no sign of changing course. When the lookout called Capt. Leask to the deck, he realized that the sound was an echo coming from an iceberg straight ahead and narrowly averted a collision.

In 1899, Capt. Leask was forced to retire from the sea. Bashed in the head with a marlin spike by a steward he caught stealing liquor, his health failed. As he left the deck of the ship for the last time, the captain lamented, "Poor old *Florence*, it won't be long now." Capt. Leask died of a brain tumor at age fifty-one in 1902, having lived to see his prophecy come true.

Very Hard Rowing

On her last voyage, the *City of Florence* sailed from Cardiff with twenty-eight officers and crew and a cargo of coal. After discharging the freight at Callao, Peru, she journeyed 800 miles south to load miter at Iquique in northern Chile. Miter, also known as niter or saltpeter, is a critical component of gunpowder. Valued at $60,000, the 1,800 ton payload was consigned to Balfour, Guthrie & Company of San Francisco, the same shipping agent which used the luckless *Rydal Hall*.

Despite a gale, during which Chief Officer Alexander Fyfe suffered a broken arm, the run north to the California coast was made in good time. On March 19, 1900, the weather was clear and Capt. George E. Stone had been able to take good observations until four o'clock that afternoon. Five hours later, darkness had fallen and the weather settled into an eerie calm. "There was a haze on the water that would have fooled the devil himself," lookout Dick McKeever shivered. "It was a thin kind of film that one minute would make you think there was fog, and the next make you rub your eyes to wonder whether you saw anything or not."

Surprised that he hadn't picked up the Farallon Islands light, Capt. Stone ordered Third Officer William Thompson aloft for a sighting. "I went aloft and saw the breakers. I got to the deck in a hurry and reported to the captain," Thompson declared. "When he sent me aloft again to make sure, I heard the cry, 'Breakers Ahead.' Almost before I got to the deck again, the ship struck."

The *City of Florence* slammed into the rocks at Half Moon Bay, caromed off, hit again, and held fast. Immediately, six feet of water rushed into the hold. The whole bottom had nearly been torn out of the ship. "Judging from the sound, she must have gone on a rock but slipped off into deep water again. I thought the ship would go down," a dismayed Capt. Stone said later. "I ordered the crew to the pumps. We might as well have tried to pump out the ocean. In about two minutes, ten feet of water was in the hold, and she had taken on a decided list."

With no hope for the ship, the captain ordered the boats lowered. He and eighteen of the crew occupied one lifeboat, while another held Second Mate Inold and the remaining eight crewmen. "Everything was afloat in the cabin so the officers could not save anything. The men secured their effects and got them into the boats," Capt. Stone reported. "After getting away from the ship's side, we found ourselves in a sea of breakers. We were surrounded by them and every moment we were in danger of being engulfed. After some very hard rowing, we got clear."

Befuddled by the Coastline

By morning, the *City of Florence* had vanished. The survivors rowed north, assuming that they were south of San Francisco. At mid-day, the

In 1900, the City of Florence *slammed into the rocks at Half Moon Bay. Newspaper headlines such as these told of her demise.* San Francisco Chronicle.

hapless group had seen nothing to indicate they were anywhere near the Golden Gate. Capt. Stone had been to this coast only once before, twenty-seven years ago. With his charts still aboard the sunken ship, the befuddled captain felt very much "asea." Having come to the conclusion that they must be north of San Francisco, he ordered the crew to row south.

Despite his unfamiliarity with the local coastline, Capt. Stone received praise for his poise during the crisis. "The captain was wonderfully cool and collected throughout," Third Officer Thompson acknowledged. "He gave the order to lower the boats when every chance of saving the ship was gone. We all had a close call, and it was wonderful that there was not a mishap."

Luckily, the steamer *Bonita*, bound for Santa Cruz, overtook the floundering bunch about ten miles out to sea. "The attention of the crew was attracted by a man in a boat waving a red shirt as a signal of distress," Charles G. Jaeger, a passenger aboard the *Bonita*, explained. Capt. Nicholson, the steamer's skipper, gave Capt. Stone their position and invited the crew aboard. Surprisingly, the invitation was declined.

"I wanted to get to San Francisco and decided to come on," a dogged Capt. Stone admitted. "We had nothing to eat or drink in our boats, so Capt. Nicholson gave us a three-day supply of food and water. Boy, I can tell you it tasted good. That put fresh heart in everybody."

The men were making fair headway back to the north when the tug *Alert*, sent to the rescue skippered by Capt. Joe Trewren, intercepted them and brought them safely to port. "The only reason I can give for the loss of my ship is that there must have been a strong current of which I was unaware," Capt. Stone shrugged. "The ship was at least twenty miles out of her course when she struck."

The beach where the *City of Florence* had wrecked was cluttered with broken masts and spars. According to one newspaper report, "The salvers who went from San Francisco left the wreck to the mercy of the beach combers, finding the sea had left nothing of value to them." Local residents scoured the shoreline, but not a vestige of the iron vessel's cargo appeared. Only a page from the ship's log book dated 1868 washed ashore, along with two live hogs which were taken in by a local farmer.

"It's a mystery to me how the old ship floated as long as she did," seaman McKeever said gratefully. "She is now over thirty years old, and in those days, they put the proper kind of material into a vessel. Had we been on one of the new-fangled clippers, not a man of us would have been left to tell the tale."

It was a fitting tribute to a timeworn, Clydebuilt ship.

11

ILL-FATED WARRIOR

DECEMBER 1, 1921

Although she never saw battle, USS *DeLong* was part of an elite fleet of American naval destroyers. The fight of her life came on the shores of Half Moon Bay.

Heroic Journey

When twenty-one year old George W. DeLong graduated from the U.S. Naval Academy at Annapolis, Maryland in 1865, he could not have foreseen his future place in history. Initially, his assignments were routine. After joining the Civil War steam sloop *Canandaigua* which served as part of the Navy's Mediterranean fleet, he rose through the ranks to Lieutenant.

In 1873, DeLong was an officer on USS *Juniata* during her voyage to Greenland with USS *Tigress* in search of the missing exploration ship *Polaris*. The Polaris expedition, formed by explorer Charles F. Hall, was troubled from the outset. Hall's authority over the group was resented by a large portion of the party, discipline broke down, and the expedition split into rival factions. After Hall's mysterious death from arsenic poisoning, the *Polaris* made an unsuccessful try for the North Pole and became wedged in the ice. Fourteen of the crew remained aboard and were rescued by a passing whaler. The other nineteen abandoned ship, drifted on an ice floe for six months, and were rescued by *Juniata* and *Tigress*.

Despite the dreadful outcome of Hall's expedition, DeLong was convinced of the value of Arctic exploration. Eager for further adventure, he joined New York newspaper publisher James Gordon Bennett, Jr. in planning an attempt to reach the North Pole in a ship specially strengthened to drift in the Arctic icepack. Bennett had purchased the British steam bark *Pandora* in 1876 and renamed her the *Jeannette*. He turned her over to the U.S. Navy and paid for all expenses. Under the terms of a Congressional authorization, the Navy provided officers and crew for the expedition.

Selected to command the venture, DeLong brought the *Jeannette* from Europe to San Francisco's Mare Island Navy Yard where she was massively reinforced for ice navigation. On July 8, 1879, he sailed for the Bering Strait, despite warnings from the U.S. Coast and Geodetic Survey that "nothing in the least tends to support the widely spread but unphilosophical notion that in any part of the Polar Sea we may look for large areas free of ice."

By early September, the *Jeannette* entered the ice and remained in its grip for almost two years. Crushed by the ever-increasing pressure of the ice, she broke open and sank in June 1881. After abandoning ship, Lt. Cdr. DeLong led his men on a heroic three month journey across the rugged ice to open water north of Siberia. There, they launched three boats that they dragged throughout their icy travels. One of the boats disappeared in a storm a few days later. Lt. Charles Chipp and seven crew became the expedition's first fatalities.

The other two craft, commanded by DeLong and by engineer George W. Melville, reached the Lena River Delta, where they landed at widely separated points. The Lena is the easternmost of the three great Siberian rivers that flow into the Arctic Ocean. Melville's party of eleven reached safety and later dispatched search parties to look for the others.

Suffering badly from frostbite, exhaustion, and hunger, DeLong and his thirteen companions struggled southward searching for a settlement. Sadly, with the exception of two men sent ahead to seek rescue, all died during October of 1881. The bodies of DeLong and nine of his men were discovered March 23, 1882 and brought back to the United States for reburial in early 1884.

The destroyer USS DeLong was named for Lt. Cdr. George W. De-Long, a naval officer and Arctic explorer. Author's collection.

The Jeanette, *Lt. Cdr. George W. DeLong's Arctic exploration vessel, sank after being trapped in the ice. DeLong and most of his men died during a heroic but unsuccessful trek over frigid terrain.* U.S. Naval Historical Center.

Nearly forty years later, the Navy launched a ship bearing the ill-fated explorer's name. Built by the New York Shipbuilding Company, the destroyer USS *DeLong* entered the water for the first time on October 29, 1918, two weeks before the end of World War I. Appropriately, Emma DeLong Mills, the grand-daughter of Lt. Cdr. George W. DeLong, christened the ship.

New York Ship

The New York Shipbuilding Company was long the dream of Henry G. Morse. Born in 1850, he graduated from the noted Rensselaer Polytechnic Institute of Troy, New York in 1871. After serving as an engineer with the Pennsylvania Railroad, Morse spent the next twenty-five years building iron bridges and tunnels for a variety of companies. His turning point came as president of the Harlan & Hollingsworth shipyard in Wilmington, Delaware. With experience heading the most prolific iron shipbuilding enterprise in America, Morse decided to begin his own company.

Garnering the financial support of famed industrialists Andrew W. Mellon and Henry C. Frick, Morse set out to build a state of the art shipyard. Nicknamed "New York Ship," the firm's location was originally intended to be on New York City's Staten Island. Ultimately, he decided on a site in Camden, New Jersey located on the Delaware River, which offered better land, rail facilities, and access to a great number of experienced shipyard workers. Ground was broken July 3, 1899 and the yard opened June 15, 1900.

The company operated according to Morse's five principles, making it the most modern and efficient shipyard in the country. First, New York Ship used the template system which called for fabrication and assembly to be done separately. Second, all major parts were prefabricated. Third, overhead cranes connected all parts of the yard for easy movement of parts. Fourth, the shipbuilding ways were roofed to avoid delays caused by bad weather. Fifth, many tasks that were traditionally completed during outfitting were now completed before launching.

New York Ship built its first vessel, the *M.S. Dollar*, in 1901 for the renowned Robert Dollar Company (Dollar Steamship Company) of San Francisco. Morse's firm would go on to build crafts of all types from car floats and barges to tankers and passenger ships. Vessels constructed for the Navy included battleships, battle cruisers, aircraft carriers, tenders, repair ships, landing craft, and destroyers such as USS *DeLong*.

Awaiting final fitting out, USS DeLong *sits amid other Navy destroyers in New York Shipbuilding Corporation's huge shipyard. Note the triple torpedo tubes on the wharf in the center foreground and destroyer smokestacks in the lower left.* U.S. Naval Historical Center.

With the expansion of the yard during World War I, New York Ship became the largest shipyard in the world. During this period, the company also began to build communities designed to attract and house an ever increasing workforce. Yorkship Village, today known as Fairview, was an example of this type of self-contained neighborhood.

"Yorkship and the other improvised towns for war workers are not going to be a mere conglomeration of rude shanties, like the mushroom towns that spring up around mines in the Far West," architect Electus D. Litchfield declared. "They are to be things of beauty. Yorkship will embody all that is attractive in our old Colonial style of architecture — yet be up to date in everything; it will be a town that will give the workers new zest for the morrow's work when they troop home of an evening."

In World War II, the company supplied heavy combatant ships for the U.S. Navy. In all, seventy ships built by New York Ship saw service during the war. As military contracts dried up in the mid-sixties, the company could not continue. The last ship to leave the yard, the submarine USS *Guardfish*, was completed in May 1965. Shortly thereafter, the firm went out of business.

"The New York Shipbuilding Company has played an important part in the contribution to American shipbuilding and to the defense of the nation in two world wars," one account stressed. "In the peacetime years, as one of the three largest shipyards in the United States, the company has contributed substantially to the commercial needs of the country's cargo, passenger and tanker lines, and has built a large number of the naval ships of many different classifications."

Henry G. Morse, New York Ship's guiding force, died unexpectedly in 1903, having seen only the beginning of his dream come true.

"Second to None"

Small, lean, and graceful, USS *DeLong* was meant to be part of "a fleet second to none." The 1,090 ton destroyer was designed with a flushed deck containing four stacks. Armament consisted of four, 4-inch, fifty caliber naval guns, and twelve 21-inch torpedo tubes.

Sailing from New York in November of 1919, *DeLong* was sent to Guantanamo Bay Naval Base at the southeastern tip of Cuba. The U.S. had secured the base and a fine land-locked harbor through a treaty signed with Cuba in 1903. Here, the Atlantic fleet engaged in fleet maneuvers and target practice. Later, *DeLong* undertook patrol duties in the Caribbean and off Central America.

The following year, *DeLong* proceeded to San Diego, where she sailed in maneuvers and torpedo practice until placed in reserve. After overhaul at San Francisco's Mare Island Naval Yard, she returned to her base at San Diego on July 26, 1921 and began operating with fifty percent of her usual crew complement.

Later that year, *DeLong* was en route to San Francisco with five other destroyers when she was thrown off course by heavy off-shore swells. Lost in a thick early morning fog, the vessel ploughed over two rocky ledges onto a sandy beach one mile south of Half Moon Bay.

The stricken ship flooded with six feet of water, a large gash puncturing her side. Lt. Cdr. F.L. Johnson, *DeLong*'s skipper, sent a hurried distress message to San Francisco before the wireless went dead. Not knowing if the "SOS" was heard, the commander sent four men out in an effort to reach shore. The boat capsized and all were thrown into the violent surf. Somehow, everyone managed to swim the two hundred yards to the beach.

DeLong's companion destroyer, USS *Frederick*, had received the distress call and relayed it to San Francisco. Lifeguards, tugs, and the destroyer *Badger* rushed to the scene. Unfortunately, the prevailing fog hindered efforts to locate the wrecked vessel. It was not until noon that rescuers finally found the stricken ship.

By then, the destroyer was so far in on the beach that the tugs had difficulty getting in close enough to place tow lines aboard. In addition, they concluded, "There is a chance that the plates have been so badly wrenched that once the hull is freed from the sand, the water will pour into the ship." USS *DeLong* remained hopelessly grounded in shallow water, within a stone's throw of dry land.

After standing by for several hours, the rescue vessels were recalled. Meanwhile, Rear Admiral Charles F. Hughes of the Twelfth Naval District arrived by truck to personally supervise a second rescue effort from shore. With him came Capt. Norman Nelson and ten surf men from the Golden Gate Coast Guard Station.

The rescue team lost no time in rigging up a breeches buoy to begin bringing the sailors ashore. A breeches buoy is a circular lifebuoy, attached to a pair of rubber pants, used by lifesaving crews to extract people from wrecked vessels. The buoy was secured by firing a line from a small onshore cannon, known as a Lyle Gun, onto the ship's deck. To effectively use the breeches buoy took skill and timing. Each

In 1921, USS DeLong *wrecked when she ploughed over two rocky ledges onto a sandy beach at Half Moon Bay.* U.S. Naval Historical Center.

A rescue team rigged up a breeches buoy, like this one, to bring stranded sailors ashore from the wrecked USS DeLong. *Grand Haven Tribune.*

member of the rescue crew had to know exactly what to do at the proper time or the entire operation could become a disaster.

In the pounding surf with waves breaking high over the disabled craft, the 115 members of *DeLong*'s crew were hoisted to safety. "The entire town of Half Moon Bay turned out to help," newspapers reported. "Fires were built on the beach to warm the men as they were brought to shore. Women made coffee and sandwiches. Supplies were furnished by A.W. Fontes of the town garage who sailed the seas on a destroyer during World War I."

Reduced to Scrap

Members of the rescue crew also rigged up a cable from a high bluff near the wreck to USS *DeLong* and the work of salvaging guns, munitions, machinery, and parts began. With storm warnings issued for the vicinity, the crew rushed the salvage work. The waves beat relentlessly over the crippled ship, putting the crew in constant peril.

"At low tide, *DeLong*'s bow is completely out of water," one report said. "As a result of the heavy swells which have been pounding the ship, two sea anchors attached to the stranded ship will be put out in an attempt to steady her and prevent her from being further wedged in her sandy position."

Within a few days, most of the Navy's equipment was removed and the destroyer's hull was declared not worth repairing. Much of the machinery and interior fixtures already removed were transferred to other destroyers. The Navy contracted with Hanlon Dry Dock & Shipbuilding of Oakland to salvage what remained. The *Homer*, one of Hanlon's wrecking steamers, succeeded in pulling the hulk off the beach. On December 17, *DeLong* was dragged back into deep water and towed to the naval base at Mare Island.

A board of inquiry was convened aboard USS *Melville* at Mare Island to uncover the reason for the mishap. Ironically, *Melville* was named for George W. Melville, who commanded the only group to survive the Arctic expedition led by George W. DeLong when they left San Francisco on the *Jeannette*.

Fifteen witnesses who were called during the investigation exonerated Lt. Cdr. Johnson of any wrongdoing. According to the board's report, "The vessel had but one radio operator available for duty who was compelled to work long watches without relief. A small crew prevented the ship from being handled properly."

Despite the Board's finding, others speculated that the fog and the minimal keeper crew at Point Montara may have contributed to the mishap. "This station is one of the most important in the approach to San Francisco harbor. Dense fogs prevail, often lasting several days at a time," a U.S. Lighthouse Board report stated. "It has frequently been necessary to send additional help to the station to maintain necessary watches. A third keeper is urgently required."

In February 1922, USS *DeLong* was towed to Thomas Crowley's Shipyard in Oakland. Established in 1892, the company's motto was: "Anything, Anywhere, Anytime, on Water." There, over the next fifty days, she was slowly reduced to scrap.

USS *DeLong* sailed on, as repair parts for other ships.

12

EXPERIMENTAL JOURNEY

SEPTEMBER 13, 1946

Perhaps the most unique cargo to cross the shores of Half Moon Bay and Point Montara was carried by *YP-636*. The Navy patrol vessel wrecked while carrying radioactive fish specimens taken after atom bomb tests at Bikini Atoll.

"The Gadget"

Seeking an end to World War II, the American government spent more than two billion dollars developing a powerful secret weapon. Known as the Manhattan Project, a group of prominent scientists headed by Dr. J. Robert Oppenheimer were charged with creating the world's first atom bomb.

The bomb was tested on the plains of northern New Mexico in the early morning hours of July 16, 1945. "The Gadget," as it was code-named, burst through the still-dark skies in a white blaze, exploded into an orange fireball, and settled into a mushroom cloud of radioactive vapor at 30,000 feet. Beneath the cloud lay a wasteland.

Oppenheimer commented, "The atomic bomb made the prospect of future war unendurable. It has led us up those last few steps to the mountain pass; and beyond there is a different country."

Ten days later, the United States, China, and Britain issued the Potsdam Proclamation calling for Japan's unconditional surrender. When Japan refused, the U.S. felt there was no alternative but to unleash their secret weapon. On August 6, 1945, the *Enola Gay*, a B-29 Superfortress bomber, dropped an atom bomb on Hiroshima killing more than 70,000 people. Three days later, another atom bomb devastated Nagasaki. Japan surrendered on August 15th.

In 1947, Oppenheimer became Director of the Institute for Advanced Study at Princeton. Also serving as Chairman of the General Advisory Committee to the Atomic Energy Commission, he warned against entering an arms race with Russia and against developing the even more powerful hydrogen bomb.

His views earned him enemies who concocted charges of disloyalty. Following a hearing before the Atomic Energy Commission in 1954, Oppenheimer's security clearance was rescinded. "Ironically, this enhanced his fame," one biographer noted. "Where once he had been known as the 'father of the atomic bomb,' he now became even more Promethean — a martyred scientist, like Galileo."

Operation Crossroads

Despite Oppenheimer's optimism about ending world warfare, the U.S. continued its atomic testing. Operation Crossroads was a test series designed to study the effects of nuclear explosions on naval vessels, airplanes, and animals. A fleet of seventy-one surplus and captured ships anchored in the Bikini Atoll lagoon in the Marshall Islands were used as targets.

Most of the islands consisted of little more than a coral reef that emerged above sea level only during the lowest tides. These islands, called atolls, had a circular or oval shape surrounding a central lagoon, outlining the tops of volcanic cones that rose 15,000 feet from the ocean floor.

In most cases, the original volcano had eroded away, leaving only narrow bands of living coral filled with sand and limestone. Sections of the atolls could support scrubby vegetation and even palm trees, but very few people. The islands were thousands of miles away from Hawaii as well as distant from more densely populated areas in Asia. Bikini Atoll was home to 162 inhabitants. The American government moved these people to another island with plans to return them when testing was complete.

A support fleet of more than 150 ships provided quarters, experimental stations, and workshops for the 42,000 personnel involved in conducting the tests. The Survey Unit included *YP-636*, a humble but essential vessel used for training and research. The designation YP, which stands for Naval District Yard Patrol boat, has been in use since 1920. However, craft serving in this role were used as early as World War I. Many were small launches or private yachts commandeered for the duration of hostilities.

The first YPs were constructed for the Coast Guard. Designed by John Trumpy of the John H. Mathis Shipyard in Camden, New Jersey, the vessels were originally used as inshore patrol boats. Built in the 1920s and taken over by the Navy between 1933 and 1936, these 75-footers made 16 knots and were armed with a 20mm cannon and dual depth-charge tracks. "Their sleek, yacht-like lines, narrow beam and plumb bow were portents of Trumpy's future works," one source maintained, "and by all accounts, they had good sea-keeping abilities, if a bit rolly, while performing their duties with distinction."

Established in 1906, the John H. Mathis Shipyard was known far and wide for its high quality yachts and ships. After a six-year stint at the New York Shipbuilding Company, John Trumpy joined Mathis as a designer. He created nearly fifty yachts for clients such as the DuPonts, the Guggenheims, and the Dodge and Chrysler families, setting a new industry standard for excellence. In 1925, he designed the *Sequoia* which later served eight U.S. Presidents beginning with Franklin D. Roosevelt.

During World War II, the Navy planned to use YPs solely as minesweepers but soon recognized their versatility. In addition to transporting troops, munitions, gasoline, food, and mail, "Yippies" were widely used in the Pacific to navigate over shallow atolls, tow damaged ships, and rescue downed pilots. Thirty-seven YPs were lost due to enemy action, accidents, and other "perils of the sea." To fill the void, a new, larger class of YP was built, considered by many to be the true essence of a patrol vessel and among the best-built wooden-hulled naval vessels. Launched on January 27, 1945, *YP-636* was among them.

Bombs Away

The atomic bomb tests at Bikini Atoll consisted of two detonations, a low altitude test and a shallow water test. Vice Admiral W.H.P. Blandy, Commander of Operation Crossroads, declared, "The bomb will not

Built by John H. Mathis & Company, patrol boats like YP-636 were considered to be among the best-built wood naval vessels. Phil Cohen.

start a chain-reaction in the water converting it all to gas and letting the ships on all the oceans drop down to the bottom. It will not blow out the bottom of the sea and let all the water run down the hole. It will not destroy gravity. I am not an atomic playboy, as one of my critics labeled me, exploding these bombs to satisfy my personal whim."

In June of 1946, a B-29 dropped a bomb on the "target fleet." Although the bomb fell two thousand feet short of the anticipated mark, five vessels were sunk. Surprisingly, given the intensity of the blast, the radioactivity it caused had only a transient effect and within a day nearly all the surviving ships were safely re-boarded for examination.

In July, another bomb was suspended beneath an old vessel, anchored in the midst of the derelict fleet, and detonated. The underwater blast sank, capsized, or severely damaged sixteen ships. As a result of the explosion, the floor of the lagoon was seriously contaminated with a layer of radioactive sludge which had long-term environmental consequences.

In addition, a wall of radioactive spray surged over the target fleet. Most of the ships could not be inspected for several weeks, after which a program of decontamination was begun. By August, the support fleet also became contaminated by low-level radioactivity in marine growth found on the ships' hulls and in the seawater piping systems.

"The test proved to have much more serious after-effects because the radioactive material was mixed with the water and the ships were contaminated," Rear Admiral Robert Conard, one of the test team's medical doctors, acknowledged. "The algae had taken up radioactivity from the water and the sides of the ships became radioactive. We had to move people for sleeping in toward the center of the ship so they wouldn't get irradiated."

The decision was made to stop work in Bikini and tow the surviving target fleet to a nearby island where the work could be done in uncontaminated water. When the work was completed, eight ships and two submarines were towed to the U.S. and Hawaii for further study.

Beyond evaluating the ships, scientists were actively monitoring fish species. Prior to the initial detonation, they collected 2,000 fish from the atoll. Between the first and second blasts, they collected 2,000 more, and another 1,400 following the last explosion. A report written by biologist Arthur Welander described the findings, noting that none of the specimens taken within the lagoon after the tests remained entirely free of radioactive contamination.

Scientists pack radioactive fish for transport from atomic bomb tests at the Bikini Atoll. University of Washington Libraries.

Samples of some of the fish taken from Bikini lagoon were identified for further examination by the U.S. Fish and Wildlife Service laboratories at Stanford, Palo Alto, California. Reassigned to the Western Sea Frontier which was responsible for Pacific coast sea defense during the war, *YP-636* was dispatched on special assignment to deliver the specimens. On August 19, 1946, she set out for San Francisco laden with twenty-five tons of frozen radioactive fish.

Unlucky Friday

All went well on the voyage until Friday, September 13, 1946. Just after 3:00 A.M., *YP-636* ran aground two miles south of Half Moon Bay during a heavy fog. Initially, Lt. C.D. Bailey, the ship's skipper and a Navy veteran of nineteen years, gave orders to back the ship off the rocks and into navigable waters. The efforts were to no avail.

YP-636 was hopelessly stranded on a rocky ledge just a hundred yards from dry land. Her hull had been ripped wide open. Lt. Bailey admitted later, "I didn't know that we were off course until we hit. We were in between rocks and couldn't get out because of the swells."

Around 7:00 A.M., he ordered sixteen members of the crew ashore. Fortunately, all reached the beach without further mishap. Three hours later, the eleven men who remained aboard were forced to abandon ship. Approaching shore, their lifeboat capsized, tossing them all into the gurgling surf. A gunner's mate, R. H. Peterson, was dashed into the side of the boat and fractured his head. Luckily, the water was shallow and Peterson waded safely to shore with the rest of his crewmates. According to one account, "the water-soaked sailors calmly stood in their shorts drying uniforms over driftwood fires."

A local resident, Mrs. Divecchio, was the first to hear the ship as it neared the shore with its fog whistle blowing constantly. She phoned Half Moon Bay Constable Fred Simmons who located the stricken craft and called the Sheriff's Office in Redwood City. Rescue squads rushed to the scene, equipped with blankets, stretchers, and other gear to assist the drenched crew.

After radioing Naval headquarters in San Francisco, Lt. Bailey attempted to steady the ship by shooting a breeches buoy line aboard. His efforts failed. "The 128 foot craft, rolling in the surf a hundred yards offshore and taking a heavy pounding, was lying on its starboard side by the afternoon," one report noted. "The mast whipped back and forth and spectators on the beach feared it might break in two."

Carrying radioactive fish samples from Bikini Atoll in 1946, YP-636 ran aground at Half Moon Bay. California Today.

The Navy dispatched a patrol blimp to observe the area and to report if it was possible to re-float the vessel. Further efforts to salvage the battered *YP-636* were delayed for fear it was radioactive. Under the direction of Rear Admiral Van Hubert Ragsdale, Deputy Commander of the Western Sea Frontier, Coast Guard engineers took Geiger counter tests to detect radiation. Guards were dispatched to secure the wreck and its cargo and to protect curious onlookers from possible contamination.

The raging sea swallowed the fish samples like a ravenous seal. Once the site was deemed safe from radioactivity, Navy crews and scientists from the U.S. Fish and Wildlife Service gathered in the few remaining fish specimens. Loaded onto refrigerated trucks, they were transported to cold storage vaults at the Treasure Island Navy Base.

Preliminary experiments on the radioactive fish were scheduled at the laboratories of the San Francisco Academy of Sciences before their final transfer to Stanford. Oscar E. Sette, a pioneer in marine fisheries research and head of Stanford's laboratory, acknowledged, "The ability to gain any scientific knowledge from the fifty to one hundred fish now in refrigeration lockers depends of the degree of disintegration which has taken place."

Unfortunately, only a mere two percent of the unique $20,000 cargo was salvaged. As the only supply of pelagic, or ocean-roaming, fish collected after Operation Crossroads, it was considered a "terrific scientific loss."

The unlucky *YP-636* lay abandoned on the reef where she struck. "The beach was covered with shredded wood as the bottom began to break up," one observer commented. Pounded to pieces, she just slipped away, bit by bit.

13

OTHER SHIPWRECKS

B etween 1851 and 1940, thirteen other shipwrecks occurred near Half Moon Bay and Point Montara. They include the *Republic*, an early steamship delivering mail to California; the cargo steamer *Roma*, a sister ship of the famous *Leelanaw*; the passenger steamer *Nippon Maru*, the first Japanese liner to provide service across the Pacific Ocean; and the steam schooner *Gray's Harbor*, one of the many fine vessels crafted by noted shipbuilder John Lindstrom.

Republic – October 5, 1851

The launching of the *Republic* at Baltimore, Maryland in 1849 was hailed as "the inauguration of steamship communication with Southern ports." The vessel departed on her initial journey to Charleston, South Carolina "with a full cargo of freight and a number of passengers."

Later, she ventured to California carrying mail for the United States Mail Steamship Company. One voyage went awry just short of her intended destination. As dense fog shrouded the coastline, the *Republic* struck the rocks at Point Montara. Although Capt. Hudson prepared to beach the ship, help arrived and she was towed to San Francisco for repairs.

145

Built by J.A. Robb, the *Republic* was a wooden sail and side-wheel steamship. She was 206 feet long, 30 feet wide, and measured 852 tons. The vessel was owned by George Law, a financier and president of U.S. Mail. The steamer sailed until 1870 when she was condemned.

Maggie Johnston & Mary Martin — 1863

Two schooners, about which there is little information, stranded at Half Moon Bay during the same year. Their fates are unknown.

Alert — November 28, 1868

Another schooner, plying the coastal trade, ran aground at Half Moon Bay five years later. Valued at $6,000, she carried no insurance and was a total loss. The vessel was owned by Mark and Archibald Harloe and Thomas Burns.

William Taber — 1871

The steamer *William Taber* came to grief on the reefs at Half Moon Bay and was later saved "with considerable difficulty." She was remodeled and refitted, placed under the command of Capt. J.C. Bogart, and put into service on the coastal trade route between San Francisco and Eureka. "She was well patronized," a local newspaper said, "helping to get people and their produce to market at reasonable rates."

San Ramon — February 1, 1875

Bound for San Blas, Mexico from San Francisco, the steamship went ashore at Half Moon Bay. Commanded by Capt. Powlers, she was salvaged and taken to San Francisco for repairs.

Ada May – October 27, 1880

The *Ada May* was one of several hundred small sailing schooners serving coastal lumber ports from Seattle to the Mexican border. Owned by the S.H. Harmon Lumber Company, her regular run was between San Francisco and Bowen's Landing in Gualala, eighty-six miles to the north.

Bowen's Landing was located less than two miles northwest of the Gualala River. It was connected by railway with sawmills on the river and exported considerable lumber, ties, shingles, and tanbark. "A reef projecting a short distance westward from the point breaks the force of the swell for vessels loading at the moorings," the *Pacific Coast Pilot* warned. "Local knowledge is necessary on account of several sunken rocks in the approaches."

Skippered by Capt. Johnson, the 84-ton vessel left Bowen's Landing on October 26, 1880 laden with 120,000 feet of lumber. For hours, the schooner wended her way through increasingly dense fog. Straining to identify familiar landmarks as darkness fell, and hoping that he was near the Golden Gate, the captain turned the ship eastward.

Just before 3:00 A.M. on October 27th, Capt. Johnson steered his ship onto the rocks at Point Montara. Like other captains who wrecked in the area, he had mistaken the Point Montara fog signal for the one at Point Bonita. Valued at $5,000 the fourteen-year-old schooner was a total loss. She was sold by the State Investment Insurance Company to parties at Point Montara for a nominal sum.

Roma — September 21, 1908

The steel cargo steamer *Roma* suffered a long but rocky career. Built by J.L. Thompson & Sons in 1889, she was sold to the newly formed Rowland & Marwood Steamship Company. The vessel had a length of 309 feet, a beam of 41 feet, a depth of 21 feet, and measured 2,164 tons. The *Roma*'s builder and owner were both prominent firms in English shipping.

The Thompson family was influential in British commerce from the 1840s, when Robert Thompson established a shipping yard with his three sons. Over time, Thompson's eldest son, Robert, Jr., assumed control of the firm. When Robert, Jr. died in 1860, his son, Joseph Lowes Thompson, assumed control, changing the venture's name to J.L. Thompson & Sons in 1875. The successful enterprise built more than 100 wooden ships as well as iron and steel steamers.

Founded in 1890, the Rowland & Marwood Steamship Company was another distinguished firm. The primary partners, John Rowland and Christopher Marwood, both had experience in ship ownership and management. Rowland had been a partner in Robinson & Rowland from 1880 until the dissolution of the partnership in 1888. Marwood was manager of the International Steamship Company. From 1886, the

Built by Joseph Lowes Thompson, standing to the far left, the cargo steamer Roma *wrecked at Point Montara in 1908.* George H. Graham.

pair had also jointly managed steamships belonging to J.H. Barry & Company.

Launched from her hailing port in New York, the *Roma* seemed unlucky from the start. While loading wheat at Galveston, Texas, she was stranded during the great hurricane of 1900. The storm was the deadliest natural disaster to ever strike the United States, generating winds of 135 miles an hour and killing 8,000 people.

The following year, the *Roma* was purchased by the Saginaw Steamship Company, the owners of the *Leelanaw*. The vessel was refloated and refitted to carry oil in bulk and to burn liquid fuel rather than coal.

In 1905, while the *Roma* was carrying oil from Port Arthur, Texas to Marcus Hook, Pennsylvania, she was damaged by floating ice on the Delaware River. She was sent to the shipyard of John Roach, one of America's most noted shipbuilders, where she underwent repairs. Later that year, she was purchased by the Union Steamship Company, a subsidiary of the Union Oil Company of California.

Further difficulties awaited the troubled ship. On September 19, 1908, the *Roma* sailed with a full cargo of oil from San Pedro, California for San Francisco under the command of Capt. J. M. Lane. Forty hours later, dense fog compelled Capt. Lane to reduce speed.

Creeping along the curtained coast, the captain kept the whistle blowing, listening for other vessels that might be in his vicinity. By 7:00 A.M. on September 21st, the current and the reduced speed had driven the vessel east of her course toward Point Montara. With a sudden jolt, the *Roma* screeched onto the reef and came to an abrupt halt.

"A sudden inrush of water told Capt. Lane that a hole had been ripped into the bow. He ordered the pumps started and directed the engine room to keep up full speed astern," one account said. "Shortly, the *Roma* backed off the reef into deep water. The tanker returned to her course, leaving a trail of oil to mark her progress."

Later that afternoon, the vessel eased her way into San Francisco Bay where the Union Oil Company held their storage tanks. There, with pumps working continuously to keep her afloat, the *Roma*'s cargo was discharged. She moved on to nearby Hunter's Point for repairs where several bow plates were replaced and her bottom repainted.

The *Roma* continued to sail as a Union Oil tanker until 1915. Transferred to a succession of owners, she was renamed several times (*Tamesi*, *Riva Adriatica*, *Lina*) and finally broken up in 1931.

Nippon Maru — October 22, 1919

With several hundred passengers aboard, the *Nippon Maru* lost her bearings in the fog and struck a reef north of Half Moon Bay. "Operating a first class service," the vessel was the first liner designed for the Toyo Kisen Kaisha Steamship Company (TKK).

In 1899, her maiden voyage from Yokohama to San Francisco marked the first Japanese liner service across the Pacific. With a length of 440 feet, a width of 50 feet, and measuring over 6,000 tons, she was the largest ship to enter San Francisco up to that time.

Established by prominent businessman Asano Soichiro in 1896, TKK was popularly known as the Oriental Steamship Line. The company ran three transpacific ships between the Far East and California with visits to Hong Kong, Shanghai, Nagasaki, Kobe, and Honolulu. All were built by noted British shipbuilder James Laing.

Soichiro used a common Japanese convention in naming his new liners. The word "maru," meaning circle, was intended as a good luck charm that would allow the ship to leave port, travel the world, and return home. Thus, a completed circle was formed, bringing the ship back to its origin unharmed. The charmed name held the *Nippon Maru* in good stead.

TKK had little competition until 1902 when the Pacific Mail Steamship Company introduced the steamers *Korea* and *Siberia* which outclassed anything else in the Pacific trade. Between 1904 and 1905, the *Nippon Maru* and her sister liners were used for military purposes during the brief Russo-Japanese War. After hostilities ended, the vessels returned to their transpacific route and also began a new service to South America.

When the *Nippon Maru* grounded just after daybreak on October 22, 1919, she was sighted by a local fisherman known as Capt. Hank. Racing back to shore, he sent word to the Merchant's Exchange in San Francisco which dispatched tugs and life savers to the scene. Local newspapers commented, "The incident caused great excitement on the coastside."

Fortunately, the sea was smooth with light swells. "This raised and lowered the vessel and the hull pounded a bit upon the rocks and sand," one observed noted. "On either side were jagged rocks, but the *Nippon* was berthed exactly between them. Either one would have caused the vessel's destruction if struck squarely."

After assessing the situation, officers decided that the vessel was in no danger. The 445 passengers, which included fifty children, were told

Stranded at Half Moon Bay in 1919, the Nippon Maru *pioneered passenger liner service from Japan across the Pacific.* Bjorn Larsson.

The Toyo Kisen Kaisha Steamship Company, which operated the Nippon Maru, *was popularly known as the Oriental Steamship Company.* Bjorn Larsson.

that breakfast could be resumed. As a precaution, toddler June Harley bundled her dolly against the cold with an extra sweater. She needn't have worried. Within three hours, Capt K. Ocasaki steered the big liner off the reef under her own power.

This was not the first time the vessel had encountered difficulties. In December of 1899, Honolulu's chief microbiologist reported that plague had arrived in Hawaii. Apparently, the neophyte *Nippon Maru* had docked there in the summer with an infected corpse.

On another trip to Honolulu in 1912, the *Nippon Maru* narrowly escaped serious disaster. When a cargo of coal shifted during heavy seas, Miss M. Page of Berkeley, California was hurled into the water. Standing nearby was Ruth Ragan, a traveling companion and an official of the Young Women's Christian Association in Yokohama.

"Miss Ragan threw off her wraps and followed the girl into the water," a local newspaper reported, "and being an excellent swimmer, held her up until a boat from the *Nippon Maru* pulled them both out."

In 1920, the *Nippon Maru* was sold to Compania Sud Americana de Vapores (CSAV) of Chile and renamed the *Renaico*. In 1926, she began serving as a depot ship at Iquique, Chile and was scrapped three years later.

Gray's Harbor — 1922

The 659-ton steam schooner *Gray's Harbor*, built in 1907 by John Lindstrom at Aberdeen, Washington, wrecked near Point Montara. The vessel, 172 feet long and 38 feet wide, was partially salvaged by her owners, Sudden & Christenson of San Francisco.

Lindstrom established a ten-acre shipyard at Gray's Harbor in Aberdeen in 1898 where he built sailing vessels and steamships. Known for its fur trading, logging, and fishing industries, Gray's Harbor was advantageously situated near the Pacific Ocean less than fifty miles west of Olympia. According to one source, Lindstrom "built more steam schooners than any other man on the coast."

He was also the first shipbuilder on the Pacific Coast to launch vessels "bow on," or by the forward end of the craft. Traditionally, ships were launched "end on," or stern first, down an inclined shipway. The "side launch," whereby ships enter the water broadside, came into nineteenth-century use on inland waters, rivers, and lakes, and was given major impetus by the World War II building program.

John Lindstrom, who constructed the Gray's Harbor, *was said to have built more steam schooners than anyone else on the Pacific Coast.* Christopher Lindstrom.

During the Prohibition Era, the Gray's Harbor *experienced occasional brushes with law enforcement officials while carrying illegal shiploads of whiskey.* Christopher Lindstrom.

While Lindstrom was an honorable man, it seems that some of the schooner's crew were enticed into the shady business of transporting illegal liquor. Between 1920 and 1933, Prohibition was in effect, banning the manufacture, transportation, sale, and use of all alcoholic beverages. "Now, it was perfectly legal for skippers to carry their usual gallon of whiskey on board for medicinal purposes," one old salt acknowledged, "but the law put its foot down on shiploads of whiskey."

Unfortunately, the *Gray's Harbor* had several brushes with the law. Once, forty-five quarts of illicit brew were confiscated by local authorities. One December, holiday spirits suffered a setback when twenty cases of whiskey were discovered hidden in the quarters of the captain and first mate.

Californian — January 10, 1932

Built in 1930 at Tacoma, Washington, the newly minted *Californian* sprang a leak and foundered near Half Moon Bay. Although assistance was sent to rescue the captain and nine crew, the 74-ton trawler couldn't be saved.

Virginia — December 4, 1932

The 68-ton fishing vessel *Virginia* burned at the water's edge off Half Moon Bay. Owned by Capt. Sam Sellito of Monterey, California, the ship was built in 1929 and valued at $35,000.

Jugo Slavia — November 10, 1940

The *Jugo Slavia*, an 80-ton fishing vessel, foundered two miles southeast of Point Montara. The captain and eleven crew escaped unharmed. Owned by Frank Breskovich, the ship was built at Los Angeles, California in 1928.

EPILOGUE

Over the years, lighthouse towers and lighthouse keepers have fulfilled many missions. In peacetime, they guided mariners on the open sea. In wartime, they were part of the country's early-warning system.

Lighthouse Lookout Station

During World War II, the beacons of every lighthouse in the nation were extinguished to protect the nation's borders from possible attack. The U.S. Coast Guard, which had assimilated the U.S. Lighthouse Service in 1939, established beach patrols and lookout stations at many of the sites.

Point Montara formed part of the lookout network along California's coast. Seaman First Class Arthur Harris Smith, Jr., who served at nearby Año Nuevo Island as a member of a Coast Guard lookout crew declared, "Everyone was scared stiff."

The area was protected by various military units, including a coast artillery mobile unit, and a K9 Corps with men and dogs that patrolled the beaches. The site also served as a naval training base. The Navy operated an anti-aircraft school near Point Montara where thousands of recruits trained in shooting live rounds at targets off the coast. Beach landings were practiced as well.

Every lookout station was manned twenty-four hours a day, seven days a week. While one crew member was on liberty, the others each worked in shifts of four hours on, eight hours off. The lookout crew had three primary duties: to detect and observe enemy vessels and airplanes operating in coastal waters; to transmit information on these craft to command headquarters; and to report attempts of landings by the enemy. "Using binoculars, we scanned the horizon for any lights, ships, or planes," Smith explained. "It all had to be reported by crank telephone to headquarters in San Francisco."

During World War II, seamen like Arthur H. Smith, Jr. served at lighthouse lookout stations such as Point Montara and nearby Año Nuevo Island. Arthur H. Smith, Jr.

Not every day was filled with wartime apprehension. Occasionally, Point Montara's principal keeper and his wife still received guests. Ed Wardell, the grandson of former keeper Nils Henry Hall, visited Keeper Dempsey and his family with his parents. His mother came bearing a roast while his father toted two bottles of homemade wine. "Back in those days you didn't visit empty handed," Wardell recalled. "The Dempseys put the roast away and sent the kids to collect a 'trash dinner.' With bucket in hand, we gathered abalone, clams, and mussels."

Laverne White, the fourth child of Walter White who was Dempsey's assistant keeper in the 1920s, shared other memories. The Whites lived upstairs while the Dempseys lived downstairs. "We had to be quiet. Keepers needed their sleep during the day," she said. "We talked in whispers. There was no slamming of doors." If the children were noisy, White heard about it from Dempsey. Laverne declared, "We caught it!"

Lifetime of Service

Throughout the 1940s and 1950s, gradual change came to Point Montara. A new keeper's duplex was built and the station was tended by three Coast Guardsmen. One of them was John E. Gonzales who served as principal keeper from 1955 to 1963. He was paid a mere $200 a month but took his duties seriously. "He was a by-the-books kind of guy," John E. Gonzales, Jr. explained. "He was definitely spit and polish."

Keeper Gonzales organized the workdays into a seamless schedule. Paperwork was handled from 8:00 to 9:00 A.M. Weekday duty shifts ran four hours on and four hours off while weekend shifts ran eight hours on and twelve hours off. "He got along with the assistant keepers, but he was the boss," John, Jr. acknowledged. "He made sure they knew what was what. One mistake was okay, but you didn't do it again."

Gonzales insisted that everything be spotless. The watch room was painted often, and smudges on the lens or glass windows were erased quickly. He also ensured that the engine room was cleaned meticulously. The red floor was perpetually glossy, and the gray pipes and white walls were always gleaming. Runners were laid down to walk through the area. "His pet peeve," John, Jr. grinned, "was anyone stepping on that sparkling floor."

Gonzales took great pride in his favorite tools — a brush and brass dustpan stamped with the words, "U.S. Lighthouse Service." Without fail, he kept the precious instruments cleaned, polished, and in good repair. "Once, the brush handle fell off so he soldered it back on," John,

Point Montara Keeper John E. Gonzales, Sr., and his wife Esther, lived at the light-house from 1955 to 1963. John E. Gonzales, Jr.

Jr., noted. "He was a man who wasted nothing." Gonzales also kept the sea chest his grandfather had salvaged from the *Rydal Hall* over 130 years earlier.

In the 1950s and 1960s, the coastside was still fairly isolated and life at the lighthouse remained bucolic. The Gonzales family shared the Victorian duplex with the first assistant keeper's family while the second assistant lived alone in a converted woodshed. An old horse barn served as the garage. Together, the families raised rabbits and chickens, tended a small vegetable garden, and fished for abalone, capazoni, mussels, and rock fish.

Traveling over dirt or gravel roads, a supply truck delivered other necessities once a month. Inspectors visited the lighthouse regularly and were invariably welcomed with coffee and cookies baked by Gonzales' wife, Esther. "She was more sociable than he was," John, Jr., commented, "and really enjoyed the visits."

"Living there was nice, but there wasn't much social life. We played cards and went dancing. Going over the hill to San Mateo, just ten miles away, for milkshakes was a big deal," John, Jr. declared. "We played on the gunnery emplacements left over from World War II. When we found old ammunition on the beach, we made a game of tossing it into the sea."

Before his final assignment at Point Montara, Gonzales served at several other California lighthouses including Fort Point in San Francisco, Piedras Blancas in Cambria, Point Vicente in Palos Verdes, Table Bluff in Eureka, and Carquinez Strait in Vallejo. When the lighthouse was automated in 1963, Gonzales retired. He was the last civilian keeper in the 12th Coast Guard District.

After a lifetime of service as a "wickie" for the U.S. Lighthouse Service and as a civilian employee of the U.S. Coast Guard, John E. Gonzales, Sr. died in 1971 just one month before his sixty-eighth birthday. John, Jr. reflected, "He was very dedicated to his job and family, was self-sufficient, and he cared."

Still Sailing

Today, an off-shore buoy has replaced Point Montara's fog signal and a small aerobeacon shines from the tower. The fourth order Fresnel lens was transferred to the San Mateo County Historical Museum and is on display in the library of the College of Notre Dame de Namur in Belmont, California.

The keepers' quarters and the fog signal building have been converted into a cozy hostel for overnight stays. Although the accommodations at Point Montara have improved over the years, foggy weather conditions still persist.

Some say that if you gaze hard enough through the mist, the specter of a stalwart old ship can be seen sailing along the horizon.

This U.S. Lighthouse Service dust pan and brush were favorite tools of Point Montara Keeper John E. Gonzales, Sr. Now family heirlooms, these artifacts are reminders of a bygone day. Author's collection.

Photo by Julie Barrow.

ABOUT THE AUTHOR

JoAnn Semones, Ph.D., boarded her first ship at age three. The voyage, made aboard the military transport vessel *E.D. Patrick*, left a lasting impression. She has loved sea sagas ever since.

Her first book, *Shipwrecks, Scalawags, and Scavengers: The Storied Waters of Pigeon Point*, was published by Glencannon Press Maritime Books in October 2007. As a consultant with the Monterey Bay National Marine Sanctuary program, she also developed concepts and text for the Pigeon Point Lighthouse Interpretive Center.

JoAnn's stories have appeared in a variety of publications, including *Mains'L Haul, Professional Mariner, Lighthouse Digest, Anchor Light, La Peninsula, Good Old Days Magazine, A Light In The Mist*, and *Surviving Magazine*, as well as in Stanford University's anthology, *Learning to Live Again*, and in the *Chicken Soup for the Soul* international book series. Visit her website at: www.gullcottagebooks.com.

Appendix A

Those Who Were Lost

Isabelita Hyne — January 8, 1856

> Captain – Calhoun
> First Mate – Beatty

Rydal Hall — October 17, 1876

> Ordinary Seaman – William Baker
> Able Seaman – Alexander Barlow
> Able Seaman – George Geoger
> Able Seaman – James Gomez
> Ordinary Seaman – George Johns
> Apprentice – Keith Selwyn
> Able Seaman – George White
> Second Mate – Hugh Williams
> Able Seaman – Charles Wilson
> Steward's Boy – William Wilson

Alice Buck — September 26, 1881

> First Mate – William Barry
> Seaman – David Black
> Second Mate – D. Crocker
> Seaman – John Gunnison

Cabin Boy – George Parker
Seaman – Charles Reader
Seaman – Patrick Welch
Unidentified – cook
Unidentified – steward

Appendix B

Lighthouse Chronology

Point Montara

1875 – fog signal installed with two-story Victorian duplex
1900 – lantern erected
1902 – new fog signal building constructed
1914 – fourth order Fresnel lens installed in wooden tower
1919 – light changed from oil to electric
1928 – conical cast iron tower erected (from Mayo's Beach)
1961 – Coast Guard constructed barracks
1970 – light automated
1980 – became a hostel

Mayo's Beach

1838 – lighthouse established at Wellfleet Harbor, Massachusetts
1857 – refitted with fourth order Fresnel lens
1881 – cast-iron tower and keeper's quarters replace original structures
1922 – light discontinued
1923 – sold at auction to a private owner
1927 – reassembled at Yerba Buena, California
1928 – moved to Point Montara

BIBLIOGRAPHY

General

Black, Frederick Frasier. *Searsport Sea Captains*. Searsport, Maine: Penobscot Marine Museum, 1960.

Jeans, Peter D. *Seafaring Lore and Legend*. New York, New York: McGraw-Hill, 2004.

Lavery, Brian. *Ship*. New York, New York: DK Publishing, Inc., 2004.

Lloyd's Register of American and Foreign Shipping. London, England: Wyman & Sons, various years.

Lloyd's Register of British and Foreign Shipping. London, England: Wyman & Sons, various years.

MacGregor, David R. *Merchant Sailing Ships: 1775-1815*. Watford, England: Argus Books, Ltd., 1980.

Marshall, Don B. *California Shipwrecks*. Seattle, Washington: Superior Publishing Company, 1978.

Martin, Wallace E. *Sail and Steam on the Northern California Coast, 1850-1900*. San Francisco, California: National Maritime Association, 1983.

Matthews, Frederick C. *American Merchant Ships*, Volumes I and II. Salem, Massachusetts: Marine Research Society, 1930.

Nelson, Sharlene and Ted. *Umbrella Guide to California Lighthouses*. Kenmore, Washington: Epicenter Press, 1993.

Paine, Lincoln P. *Ships of the World: An Historical Encyclopedia*. New York, New York: Houghton Mifflin Company, 1997.

Rogers, John G. *Origin of Sea Terms*. Mystic, Connecticut: Mystic Seaport Museum, 1985.

Roland, Alex, Bolster, Jeffrey W., and Keyssar, Alexander. *The Way of the Ship*. Hoboken, New Jersey: John Wiley & Sons, Inc., 2007.

Tate, E. Mowbray. *Transpacific Steam*. Cranbury, New Jersey: Cornwall Books, 1986.

Reports of the U.S. Lighthouse Service Board, excerpts from 1874 through 1963.

U.S. Lighthouse Service Board, excerpts from reports, 1873 to 1963.

Isabelita Hyne

"Beatty's Remains," Daily Alta California, 22 January 1856.

"Cargo of the Wrecked Barque," Daily Alta California, 15 January 1856.

Cutler, Carl C. Greyhounds of the Sea. New York, New York: Halcyon House, 1930.

Haviland, Edward K. "American Steam Navigation in China, 1845-1878," American Neptune, April 1957.

"How the Isabelita Hyne was Lost," Daily California Chronicle, 18 January 1856.

"Isabelita Hyne," Daily Alta California, 16 January 1856.

"Late from the Wreck – Bodies Ashore," Daily Alta California, 20 January 1856.

Matthews, Frederick C. American Clipper Ships, 1883-1858. Salem, Massachusetts: Marine Research Society, 1926.

"News from the Wreck," Daily California Chronicle, 14 January 1856.

Nye, Charles E. The Nye Family of America. New Bedford, Massachusetts: E. Anthony & Sons, 1903.

Shavit, David. The United States in Asia. Westport, Connecticut: Greenwood Publishing, 1990.

"Shipwrecked," Daily Alta California, 12 January 1856.

"Spent in the China Trade," New York Times, 4 March 1888.

Whipple, A.B.C. The Challenge. New York, New York: William Morris & Company, 1987.

"Wreck of the Isabelita Hyne," Daily California Chronicle, 19 January 1856.

Elfin A. Kniper

Bouchereau, L. Louisiana Sugar Report. New Orleans, Louisiana: Pelican Book & Job Printing Office, 1872.

"Half Moon Bay," Pacific Sentinel, 16 January 1862.

"Half Moon Gone Luny," Daily Evening Bulletin, 21 January 1862.

"Marine Disaster," Daily Alta California, 13 January 1862.

"Rescue of the Wrecked," Daily Evening Bulletin, 16 January 1862.

"Saga of the Side-Wheel Steamer Shubrick: Pioneer Lighthouse Tender of the Pacific Coast," American Neptune, 1976.

"Shipwreck Proves Sweet Deal," *Pacifica Tribune*, 6 February 1985.

"The *Shubrick*," *Daily Alta California*, 14 January 1862.

Silverstone, Paul H. *Civil War Navies: 1855-1883*. Annapolis, Maryland: Naval Institute Press, 2001.

Sitterson, J. Carlyle. *Sugar Country*. Lexington, Kentucky: University of Kentucky Press, 1953.

Thorp, Rosemary and Bertran, Geoffrey. *Peru:1860-1977*. New York, New York: Columbia University Press, 1978.

"United States Revenue Cutter Service," Coast Guard fact sheet, July 2007.

"Wrecked Schooner," *San Mateo County Gazette*, 18 January 1862.

"Wrecked Vessels," *Daily Evening Bulletin*, 13 January 1862.

"Wrecked Vessels," *Marysville Daily Appeal*, 15 January 1862.

Colorado

"A Panic on Shipboard," *San Francisco Evening Bulletin*, 11 November 1868.

"American Ship Starts Mail Service to China," unattributed newspaper clipping, 31 December 1866.

"An Ocean Palace on Exhibition," *New York Times*, 23 March 1865.

"Arrival of the *Colorado*," *San Francisco Evening Bulletin*, 10 November 1868.

Bishop, John L., Freedley, Edwin T., and Young, Edward. *A History of American Manufacturers: 1608 – 1860*. Philadelphia, Pennsylvania: Edward Young & Company, 1864.

Braynard, Frank O. *Famous American Ships*. New York, New York: Hastings House, 1978.

"The *Colorado*," *San Francisco Evening Bulletin*, 14 November 1868.

De La Pedraja Toman, Rene. *A History of the U.S. Merchant Marine and Shipping Industry*. Westport, Connecticut: Greenwood Publishing Company, 1994.

"Docking of the *Colorado*," *San Francisco Chronicle*, 13 November 1868.

Dunbaugh, Edwin L. and Thomas, William D. *William H. Webb: Shipbuilder*. Glen Cove, New York: Webb Institute of Naval Architecture, 1989.

"For the New Dry Dock," *San Francisco Evening Bulletin*, 11 November 1868.

"Good Use for His Wealth," *New York Times*, 17 July 1890.

Kemble, John H. *The Panama Route*. Berkeley, California: University of California Press, 1943.

"Obituary: William H. Aspinwall," *New York Times*, 19 January 1875.

"William Henry Webb," *New York Times*, 11 July 1897.

"Who was William Webb," speech given by Joseph J. Cuneo, Webb Institute Founder's Day, 7 April 2006.

Aculeo

"A Brief History of a Stormy Past," *Half Moon Bay Review Magazine*, April 2008.

"A Wreck," *San Francisco Daily Morning Call*, 19 October 1872.

"*Aculeo*," *New York Marine Register*, 23 October 1872.

"*Aculeo*," *New York Marine Register*, 30 October 1872.

"*Aculeo*," *San Mateo County Gazette*, 26 October 1872.

"*Aculeo*," *San Mateo County Gazette*, 2 November 1872.

"*Aculeo*," *San Mateo County Gazette*, 9 November 1872.

"Christmas Toys Lost," *Half Moon Bay Review*, 20 December 1979.

"The Duncans of Jordanstone and Drumfork," Clan Duncan Society manuscript, August 2008.

Department of Commerce. *U.S. Coast Pilot: Pacific Coast*. Washington, D.C.: Government Printing Office, 1917.

Fairbanks, Ressa, interview with the author, 10 December 2003.

Hanssen, Robert, interview with the author, October 2007.

"Latest from the Wreck," *San Francisco Chronicle*, 21 October 1872.

"Loss of the Ship *Aculeo*," *San Mateo County Gazette*, 26 October 1872.

Middlemiss, Norman L. *British Shipbuilding Yards*. Newcastle, England: Shield Publications, 1994.

Nottestad, Shannon, interview with the author, 20 October 2003.

"Perils of the Deep," *San Francisco Chronicle*, 19 October 1872.

"The Roydens of Frankby," *Wirral Journal*, 1986.

Semones, JoAnn, "The Shipwreck Legends of Galen Wolf," *Mains'l Haul: A Journal of Pacific Maritime History*, Fall 2006.

"The Toy Ship," a story from Galen Wolf's unpublished *Legends of the Coastside*.

"Thomas B. Royden & Co.," Red Duster, Merchant Navy Association, manuscript, 2009.

"Wrecked Ship," *San Francisco Daily Morning Call*, 21 October 1872.

Rydal Hall

"Along the Wharves," *Daily Alta California*, October 20, 1876.

"Ancient Anchor Retrieved," *Burlingame Advance-Star*, 20 February 1971.

"Cannon, Bell Recovered from Wrecked Vessel," *San Mateo County Times*, 19 September 1972.

Daunton, Martin. *Coal Metropolis: Cardiff*. Leicester, England: Leicester University Press, 1977.

"For Whom the Bell Tolls – 96 Years Later," *San Francisco Examiner*, 18 September 1972.

Gonzales, John E., interview with the author, 4 February 2009.

"Rear Admiral Casey Dead," *New York Times*, 15 August 1913.

Reilly, Mary A., "Santiago," manuscript for *Methil Heritage*, 2007.

"*Rydal Hall*," *Daily Alta California*, 19 October 1876.

"*Rydal Hall*," *New York Marine Register*, 25 October 1876.

"*Rydal Hall*," *New York Marine Register*, 1 November 1876.

"San Francisco," *New York Marine Register*, 1 November 1876.

"Ship Ashore," *Times and Gazette*, 21 October 1876.

"Ship Lost When Captain Fooled by Fog," *Pacifica Tribune*, 4 August 1982.

"The Ship *Rydal Hall*," *Daily Alta California*, 28 October 1876.

"Shipwreck," *San Francisco Chronicle*, 19 October 1876.

"Wreck of the *Rydal Hall*," *San Francisco Chronicle*, 20 October 1876.

"Wreck of the *Rydal Hall*," *Daily Alta California*, 21 October 1876.

"Wreck of the *Rydal Hall*," *San Mateo Times*, 2 October 1971.

"Wreck Vessel Sold," *San Francisco Chronicle*, 21 October 1876.

Alice Buck

"A Brave Act," *San Francisco Daily Morning Call*, 29 September 1881.

"A Midnight Wreck," *San Francisco Chronicle*, 28 September 1881.

"A Signal Instance of Bravery," *San Francisco Daily Morning Call*, 30 September 1881.

"*Alice Buck*," *San Francisco Chronicle*, 29 September 1881.

"*Alice Buck*," *New York Marine Register*, 5 October 1881.

"*Alice Buck*," *New York Marine Register*, 12 October 1881.

Caldwell, Bill. *Rivers of Fortune: Where Maine Tides and Money Flowed*. Portland, Maine: G. Gannett Publishing Company, 1983.

"Capt. Phineas Pendleton II: 79th Birthday Celebration," *Republican Journal*, 6 September 1883.

"Death of Capt. Phineas Pendleton," *Bangor Daily Whig and Courier*, 22 July 1895.

Foote, H.S. *Pen Pictures from the Garden of the World*. Chicago, Illinois: Lewis Publishing Company, 1888.

History and Commerce of New York. New York, New York: American
  Publishing Company, 1891.

Honore, Chris, "Taking the Sea," *Daily Tidings*, 30 January 2009.

"Mr. Gilman Cram's Tribute," *Bangor Daily Whig and Courier*, 22 July
  1895.

"On the Rocks," *San Francisco Daily Morning Call*, 28 September
  1881.

"Sailors Swept Away in the Wreck of *Alice Buck*," *Pacifica Tribune*, 22
  February 1984.

"Trouble Among the Wreckers," *New York Times*, 29 May 1878.

"The Wreck," a story from Galen Wolf's unpublished *Legends of the
  Coastland*.

Argonaut

"Along the Wharves," *San Francisco Daily Evening Bulletin*, 5
  November 1890.

"*Argonaut*," *New York Times Marine Register*, 12 November 1890.

"*Argonaut*," *New York Times Marine Register*, 19 November 1890.

"Asa Mead Simpson: Lumberman and Shipbuilder," *Oregon Historical
  Quarterly*, September 1967.

"At Play on Oregon's Coast," *Los Angles Times*, 11 August 2002.

"Capt. Asa M. Simpson," *Bath Daily Times*, 18 June 1906.

"Captain Asa Mead Simspon," *The Californians*, January/February
  1991.

"Clipper Ships Tied to West Coast," *San Francisco Chronicle*, 22
  October 2005.

Holland, Francis Ross. *America's Lighthouses*. New York, New York:
  Courier Dover Publications, 1988.

Hughes, John C., and Beckwith, Ryan T. *On the Harbor*. Las Vegas,
  Nevada: Stephens Press, 2005.

"Pacific Lumber King," *Bath Independent*," 23 January 1915.

Schwartz, Stephen. *Brotherhood of the Sea*. Edison, New Jersey:
  Transaction Publishers, 1986.

"The Shipwreck," *The Advocate*, 8 November 1890.

Simpson, Michael, interview with the author, 6 March 2009.

"Sweet Memories of San Diego," *Lighthouse Digest*, July 2002.

Untitled story, *Peninsula Living*, 31 October 1959.

"The Wreck," *The Advocate*, 22 November 1890.

"The Wrecked Schooner," *The Advocate*, 15 November 1890.

T.F. Oakes/New York

"Climax of the Unlucky Career of the *New York*," *San Francisco Call*, 15 March 1898.

"Custom-House in a Rude Shanty," unattributed magazine clipping, 26 March 1898.

Dillon, Richard H. *Shanghaiing Days*. New York, New York: Coward-McCann, 1961.

Druett, Joan. *Hen Frigates*. New York, New York: Simon & Schuster, 1999.

Gowlland, Gladys M. O. *Master of the Moving Sea*. Flagstaff, Arizona: J. F. Colton & Co., 1959.

"Ill-Fated Ship and Her Captain," *San Francisco Chronicle*, 15 March 1898.

"Ill-Fated Ship *New York* A Total Loss," *San Francisco Chronicle*, 15 March 1898.

Johnson, Alfred S., Bickford, Clarence A., William W. Hudson, William W. and Dole, Nathaniel H. *Cyclopedic Review of Current History*: vol.8, number 4. Boston, Massachusetts: Current History Co., 1898.

"Last of the Famous Ship *New York*," *San Francisco Evening Bulletin*, 14 March 1898.

"Launch of the *T.F. Oakes*," *New York Times*, 30 September 1883.

Morrall, June. "Anatomy of a Shipwreck," *La Peninsula*, March 1990.

"*New York*," *New York Marine Register*, 16, 23 and 30 March, 1898.

"*Oakes* Towed In," *New York Times*, 22 March 1897.

Paine, Lincoln P. *Ships of the World*. New York, New York: Houghton-Mifflin Co., 1997.

Peabody, Claire. *Singing Sails*. Caldwell, Idaho: Caxton Press, 1950.

Peabody, Claire. "Then Three Times 'Round," *The Skipper*, March 1963.

"The Red Record," *Coast Seamen's Journal*, 26 January 1898.

"Rich Cargo of the Wrecked *New York*," *San Francisco Chronicle*, 15 March 1898.

"Sinking in Her Bed of Soft Sand," *San Francisco Chronicle*, 16 March 1898.

"Tug *Reliance* Visits Wrecked Vessel," *San Francisco Chronicle*, 15 March 1898.

Earnwell/Leelanaw

"A Transport on the Rocks," *New York Times*, 25 September 1899.

"American Steamer *Leelanaw*," *New York Times*, 28 July 1915.

"Americans on *Leelanaw*," *New York Times*, 27 July 1915.

Bennett, Ira E. *History of the Panama Canal*. Washington, D.C.: Historical Publishing Company, 1915.

"Big Transport *Leelanaw* Very Badly Damaged," *San Francisco Call*, 28 September 1899.

"Cape Cod Lighthouse Mystery Solved," *Cape Cod Times*, 4 June 2008.

"Capt. Delk Foresaw Peril," *New York Times*, 27 July 1915.

"Damnable Outrage," *New York Times*, 27 July 1915.

"Germans Sink the *Leelanaw*," *New York Times*, 27 July 1915.

"*Leelanaw*," *New York Marine Register*, 4 October 1899.

"*Leelanaw* Cheats Point Montara," *Nautical Brass*, May/June 1987.

"*Leelanaw* Comes Back for Repairs," *Santa Cruz Sentinel*, 26 September 1899.

"Lighthouse Turns Out to be Bicoastal," *San Jose Mercury News*, 21 June 2008.

"Missing Cape Cod Lighthouse Located in California," Associated Press news release, 5 June 2008.

"Montara Lighthouse Mystery," *Half Moon Bay Review*, 11 June 2008.

"New England Lighthouse Thought to Have Been Destroyed Found Standing in California," *Lighthouse Digest*, June 2008.

"Ran on a Reef and Lay There for Several Hours," *San Francisco Call*, 25 September 1899.

"The Saginaw Steamship Company and Its Steamers," *American Neptune*, October 1982.

City of Florence

"A Complete Wreck," *San Francisco Chronicle*, 22 March 1900.

"Another Stout Ship Lays Her Bones on Montara Reef," *San Francisco Chronicle*, 21 March 1900.

Bone, David W. *The Brassbounder*. Whitefish, Montana: Kessinger Publishing, 1921.

"Captain Stone Testifies," *San Francisco Chronicle*, 24 March 1900.

"*City of Florence*," *Santa Cruz Morning Sentinel*, 23 March 1900.

"*City of Florence*: Schooner Loaded with Nitrate Wrecked at Half Moon Bay," *Santa Cruz Morning Sentinel*, 21 March 1900.

"Court of Inquiry," *San Francisco Chronicle*, 23 March 1900.

Dana, James D. *Manual of Mineralogy*. New Haven, Connecticut: H.H. Peck, 1868.

"Goes on the Rocks," *San Francisco Call*, 21 March 1900.

McCrorie, Ian. *Clyde Pleasure Steamers*. Greenock, Scotland: Orr, Pollock & Co., Ltd., 1986.

MacLehose, James. *Memoirs and Portraits of One Hundred Glasgow Men*. Glasgow, Scotland: MacLehose & Company, 1886.

"Shipwrecks in Fair Weather," *San Francisco Chronicle*, 22 March 1900.

USS *De Long*

"Admiral Hughes Heads Warship Salvage Effort," *San Francisco Call and Post*, 3 December 1921.

"Blame Short Crew in Wreck of Destroyer," *Coast Side Comet*, 30 December 1921.

"Company's First Launching," *New York Times*, 5 May 1901.

DeLong, Emma J. Wooten. *The Voyage of the* Jeannette. Boston, Massachusetts: Houghton, Mifflin & Company, 1884.

"H.G. Morse Dies Suddenly," *New York Times*, 3 June 1903.

"Navy Abandons Attempts to Float *DeLong*," *San Mateo County Times*, 7 December 1921.

Navy Department. *American Naval Fighting Ships*. Washington, D.C.: U.S. Government Printing Office, 1963.

New York Shipbuilding Corporation. *Fifty Years: New York Shipbuilding Corporation*. Camden, New Jersey: New York Shipbuilding Corporation, 1949.

"Officers See Hard Task to Save Warship," *San Francisco Chronicle*, 4 December 1921.

"Town of Half Moon Bay Turns Out to Aid Wrecked Destroyer Crew," *Nautical Brass*, January/February 1989.

"U.S. Destroyer Rescue Given Up," *Coast Side Comet*, 2 December 1921.

"U.S. Destroyer Rescue Given Up; Salvage Munitions," *San Francisco Call and Post*, 2 December 1921.

"U.S. Warship Menaced by Giant Waves," *Coast Side Comet*, 2 December 1921.

"Warship on Beach Near Half Moon Bay," *San Francisco Chronicle*, 2 December 1921.

"Warship Stuck in Sand Holds Against Waves," *San Francisco Chronicle*, 3 December 1921.

YP-636

"Bikini Fish Ship Wrecked," *San Francisco Chronicle*, 14 September 1946.

"Building the Bomb," *Smithsonian Magazine*, August 2005.

Felando, August J. "Errand Boys of the Pacific," *Mains'L Haul: A Journal of Pacific Maritime History*, Winter/Spring 2008.

Gonzales, John E., Jr., interview with the author, October 2008.

"Navy Patrol Craft Goes on Rocks Near Half Moon Bay," *Santa Cruz Sentinel*, 14 September 1946.

"Navy Patrol Craft Wrecked on Coast," *Half Moon Bay Review*, 19 September 1946.

"Navy Tries to Save Shipload of Bikini Fish," *San Francisco Chronicle*, 15 September 1946.

"Oral History: Operation Crossroads, Reminiscences of Rear Admiral Robert Conard," Naval Historical Center, 9 November 1993.

"Part Boat, Part Ship: The U.S. Navy YP," *Passage Maker Magazine*, 11 January 2008.

"Salvage Bikini Radioactive Fish," *Santa Cruz Sentinel*, 15 September 1946.

"Shipwrecks On Our Shore," *California Today*, 8 August 1976.

Smith, Arthur H., Jr., interview with the author, April 2008.

"Vessel Hits Reef, Spills A 'Monstrous' Cargo," *Pacifica Tribune*, 23 March 1988.

Young, Christian C. *The Environment and Science*. Santa Barbara, California: ABC-CLIO, 2005.

Republic

Marshall, Don B. *California Shipwrecks*. Seattle, Washington: Superior Publishing Company, 1978.

Scharf, John Thomas. *History of Baltimore City and County*. Philadelphia, Pennsylvania: Louis H. Everts, 1881.

Maggie Johnston, Mary Martin & Alert

Marshall, Don B. *California Shipwrecks*. Seattle, Washington: Superior Publishing Company, 1978.

William Taber

Wallace, Martin E. *Sail and Steam on the Northern California Coast, 1850-1900*. San Francisco, California: National Maritime Association, 1983.

San Ramon

Newell, Gordon. *The H.W. McCurdy Marine History of the Pacific Northwest*. Seattle, Washington: Superior Publishing Company, 1966.

Ada May

"*Ada May*," Alta California, 28 October 1880.
"*Ada May*," Morning Call, 28 October 1880.
"Fog Shrouds Schooner's Doom on Rocky Shore," *Nautical Brass*, November-December 1991.
"Wreck of the *Ada May*," *San Francisco Examiner*, 31 October 1880.

Roma

"Early American Tankers," *American Neptune*, July 1978.
"Tales of Shipwrecks," *Pacifica Tribune*, 11 February 1987.
"Rowland and Marwood Steamship Company," manuscript by Whitby Library and Philosophical Society, 2001.
"The Saginaw Steamship Company and Its Steamers," *American Neptune*, October 1982.
"Shipbuilders of Sunderland," text based on the work of George H. Graham, 2006.

Nippon Maru

"Big Japanese Liner Goes Ashore at Half Moon Bay," *San Francisco Chronicle*, 23 October 1919.
"Girl Heroine on Liner," *New York Times*, 8 February 1912.
"Sir James Laing Dead," *New York Times*, 16 December 1901.
"Steamer Goes on Rocks Near Half Moon Bay," *San Mateo News Ledger*, 22 October 1919.
"Toyo Kisen Kaisha," *The Ships List*, 10 November 2007.

Gray's Harbor

Hughes, John C. *On the Harbor*. Aberdeen, Washington: Stephens Press, 2005.
Wilhelm, Honor L. *The Coast*. Seattle, Washington: Metropolitan Press, 1903.

Californian

"*Californian*," *New York Marine Register*, 13 January 1932.

"Californian," New York Marine Register, 20 January 1932.

Virginia
"Virginia," New York Marine Register, 7 December 1932.
"Virginia," New York Marine Register, 14 December 1932.

Jugo Slavia
U.S. Department of Commerce, Bureau of Navigation. *Merchant Vessels of the United States*. Washington, D.C.: U.S. Government Printing Office, 1931, 1932, and 1941.

Index

181

Y